Love of Beauty

Love of Beauty

Copper Mountain Mandala of Odiyan

Tarthang Tulku

Dharma Publishing

Love of Beauty

Copyright © 2016 Dharma Publishing

NO PART OF THIS VOLUME MAY BE REPRODUCED
WITHOUT THE PRIOR WRITTEN PERMISSION
OF THE PUBLISHER.

Registered with the Register of Copyrights and the Library of Congress.

ISBN: 978-0-89800-106-8
LCCN: 2016961966

All Rights reserved. No part of this book, including but not limited to text, art, photographs, artwork, line drawings, charts, maps or indexes, may be reproduced, transmitted, or copied in any form or by any means electronic or mechanical, including photographic, xerographic, phonographic, or otherwise, or information storage or retrieval systems, without the express written consent of the publisher. The publisher will act to protect this copyright to the fullest extent of the national laws and applicable international conventions.

Published by Dharma Publishing
35788 Hauser Bridge Road
Cazadero, CA 95421

Printed and bound in the USA by Dharma Press

Dedication

This book is dedicated to all those
who have desired in their lives to walk the path of beauty:
may you find inspiration and encouragement
in these pages.

Odiyan and the Path of Beauty

Odiyan was founded in August of 1975. Since then it has stood at the West of the West, our beloved mandala garden, embodiment of love of beauty.

Our sense-impressions and thoughts, those precious vehicles, constitute an open opportunity, an invitation to ever-greater love and caring. If we do not take this opportunity, we can, without meaning to, realize other kinds of expressions, inviting distractions and cultivating attitudes that lead to the deterioration of nature, both the world's and our own.

Instead, meditating on beauty, we can realize beauty. In Odiyan's shining mirror, we can catch a glimpse of our own beauty reflected—if we can take the time to acknowledge our relationship, and reflect on this reflection.

For beauty is recognized. Our love of what is beautiful is a reflection; it emerges from deep within, and sees its face in the rose.

If what we love is part of us, then we, too, are worthy of love.

That line of recognition sent forth by our sense faculties—if we could appreciate it, challenge it, transform it, then the recognition of beauty could become a path of beauty, a path of self-appreciation and self-contentment, and ultimately, a path of freedom.

Love of Beauty

The Land of Odiyan

When we founded Odiyan in 1975, the setting was spectacular, but the land itself had been badly damaged. Gradually we have been able to work a transformation. Today the gardens and land of Odiyan have matured, and they exhibit remarkable beauty.

Many visitors have remarked on the transformation of Odiyan in the past decade or so, and several have asked me to reflect on how such beauty came to be. Occasionally people also ask me or the Odiyan residents for more information about what they are seeing? "What is that plant," they ask; where does it come from and when did you plant it?

Since these questions come up for many visitors, I have decided it would be worthwhile to present a comprehensive guide to the flowers, trees, plants, and shrubs of Odiyan. At the same time, I am taking this opportunity to share some of my informal reflections on Odiyan. Some of these are personal, touching on memories I have of my childhood or the early years here at Odiyan. Others relate more directly to the land, and to what it means to create beauty for the heart to appreciate, enjoy, and share with others.

I will be happy if the thoughts and information collected here deepen people's appreciation for Odiyan and help them explore for themselves the feelings that Odiyan evokes. At the same

Cherry Mall bursting into bloom before Odiyan's Central Temple

time, it serves a practical purpose to pass on information that has taken many years of hard work to accumulate, and that might otherwise be lost. After all, if we lose track of our own origins, something precious in our being falls short. If one day

Swans and ducks navigate the pond surrounding the temple mandala

the name of Odiyan is lost, its power to bring benefit to all beings will be undermined. I hope that this will not be so—that residents of Odiyan, as well as visitors, continue to cherish all aspects of the beauty and meaning this sacred realm preserves.

Thousands of yellow irises are blooming in profusion

Origin Stories

Odiyan takes its name from Oddiyana, an ancient mystic land located in the Swat Valley, which straddles present-day Pakistan and Afghanistan. The monumental Buddha statues of Bamiyan, carved out of the cliffs in the fifth and sixth centuries C.E., and only recently destroyed, are associated with this region, where Buddhist temples are known to have flourished some two thousand years ago.

Americans today carry in their minds the image of Shangri La, a secret, hidden land of profound esoteric knowledge. The story of Shangri La is fiction, based on a novel and film less than a century old. In some respects, however, Oddiyana could be considered the historic equivalent of Shangri La, a place where even the trees and plants expressed a sacred energy. For Tibetans, it holds special importance as the birthplace of Guru Padmasambhava, the founder of Buddhism in Tibet.

The ruler of Oddiyana in the time of the Buddha was King Indrabodhi. The story is told that when the King learned that the Buddha had appeared in the world, he invited him to Oddiyana. When the Conqueror had arrived and been suitably honored, the King requested teachings. With great reverence, he explained that his wish was to receive teachings that did not depend on following the gradual, monastic approach to enlightenment, for he realized that he could not follow the discipline of a renunciate and still discharge his duties as king. Instead, he asked for teachings that would reveal a way to reach the freedom of perfect enlightenment instantly, not only for himself, but for his whole kingdom.

White magnolias opening wide at the Stupa

Knowing that King Indrabodhi had a very special mind, and that he was indeed ready to receive such profound teachings, the Buddha transmitted to him instructions that would later be developed as the Vajrayana, the Diamond Vehicle of the highest teachings. Following the instructions revealed by the Enlightened One, the King, his ministers, and their retinue all attained realization.

Cheerful yellow tulips highlight the temple gardens

From that time forward, the people of Oddiyana exhibited special powers. The women of that land in particular often manifested the power of dakinis, able to fly through the air. It is said that in later times, the entire population of Oddiyana achieved realization, disappearing from the face of the earth. This seems to be a manifestation of the ability to achieve the rainbow body, a practice well known in Tibet. I have heard that other cultures may also have known of this ability to transmute the body into light, and they may have practiced it.

Spring colors of the Main temple gardens

The tradition of the rainbow body initiated in Oddiyana has continued in Tibet down through modern times. It is especially associated with Kahthog monastery, founded by Kadampa Deshek (1122-1192). Kahthog was noted in early times for its highly accomplished practitioners, who excelled in their mastery of the inner Maha, Anu, and Ati Yogas.

It is said that all five of Kadampa Deshek's principal disciples attained the rainbow body, and this tradition continued among

Pelargonium and succulants at Vairocana Garden

his followers. According to the accounts found in Tibetan histories, scores of yogins would leave the monastery each day to practice on the mountain tops. Their visualizations and mantras had extraordinary power, penetrating the very heart of existence. It is said that at times when these yogic practitioners returned to the monastery in the evening, villagers would find that their buckets of water had mysteriously been drained, a fact that in popular lore was attributed to the power of their meditation.

Orange roses in the Stupa gardens

It is said that over the centuries a hundred thousand of Kahthog's most accomplished yogins attained the rainbow body. Since as a result of this accomplishment, only the practitioners' robes would remain behind, the mountain where this happened became known as Robe Mountain.

In recent times, such accomplishments have been rare, but they have not disappeared entirely. It is widely believed that thirteen disciples of Adzom Drugpa, with whose son and Dharma heir A-'gyur Rinpoche I studied, attained the rainbow body.

Swans gliding by the yellow irises

As for what I can relate from my own experience, I once passed through Mani Khago on my way from Dzogchen to Dzongsar monasteries. On the way, I met a man who was a disciple of Jamyang Khyentse Chokyi Lodro. He told me that his father had vanished around the time that he himself was born. In Tibet, corpses were often wrapped in cloth for some time before being cremated, and he told me that when they unwrapped the cloth in which his father's body had been placed, they found only his robes and some hair. His father was a well-known practitioner, though I do not know where he received the lineage that would lead to such an attainment.

Main temple pond gardens in spring

I tell those stories here because for me they make a link to the lineage established at Oddiyana. We sometimes forget that the ordinary events of our lives connect to the fundamental forces that shape the cosmos. For instance, the way our lives unfold from birth to death is linked to the way that time and space were established—according to current scientific views—in the Big Bang. The rhythms of life on this earth, the evolution of our species, and the journey we are on as individuals are all inseparable from the laws of nature that the theory of the Big Bang manifests. Could it be possible, then, that great practitioners in the lineage of realization that traces back to Oddiyana knew how to engage a different time and space?

Maples glow at the Main Temple

Could such knowledge have made it possible for them to transcend the limits of our ordinary existence on this earth? The Mahayana Buddhist teachings speak of the Dharmakaya or Dharmadhatu as completely full and all-encompassing, with no beginning, middle, or end. For a practitioner who understands this fullness, it might be possible to invoke a different potentiality. For me, Oddiyana represents such a potentiality or possibility. In turn, this suggests to me that although we are half a world and many centuries removed from the ancient land of Oddiyana, we are not as distant in time or space as we may ordinarily imagine. That, at least, is my fantasy.

Autumn colors in the Temple gardens

There is another reason to honor the land of Oddiyana. Guru Rinpoche, the great Lotus-Born Master, took birth on Lake Dhanakosha in the northwest of Oddiyana. Later, when King Trisong Detsen and Abbot Shantarakshita encountered obstacles in establishing the Dharma in Tibet, they asked for the assistance of the Great Guru, and he granted their request, journeying to Tibet. There he subjugated the demons and marayas who were doing their best to prevent the Buddha's teachings from taking root in the Land of Snow. These efforts were successful, and the obstacles that had prevented founding the Dharma in Tibet were overcome. Without the Oddiyana

Poplars begin to show their colors around the pond

Guru, there would be no Tibetan Buddhism, and the priceless teachings preserved only in Tibet would have been lost.

Of course, the history of the Dharma in Tibet can trace its origins to a variety of influences. It goes back to the time of King Lhatotori, who received the first signs of the teachings during his reign. It continues in the seventh century, when King Songtsen Gampo established a vast empire and took the first all-important steps toward establishing the Dharma, building temples, commissioning the creation of a written language, and developing a new foundation for Tibetan society.

Approaching the Main Temple from the east

Still, it was in the eighth century, under Trisong Detsen, that the Nyingma teachings were firmly established. Through the inspired efforts of the teacher, the abbot and the king (Khen Lob Cho Sum) the vision of the Dharma upheld with such distinction by the great monastic universities of Nalanda and Vikramashila came to Tibet. Realized panditas and accomplished Tibetan lotsawas such as Vairotsana, Yeshe De, Kawa Paltseg, and Chogro Lui Gyaltsen joined together to transmit the teachings at every level.

Cherry trees show warm colors near the Stupa

Thanks to their incomparable knowledge, brought to fruition through lifetimes of dedicated study and practice, the traditions of Sutra, Shastra, and Tantra were firmly established. That lineage has continued unbroken down through the centuries: from Rongzom Mahapandita, Longchenpa, and Jigme Lingpa to Jamyang Khyentse Wangpo and Lama Mipham, and all the way down to the teachers with whom I had the remarkable good fortune to study as a young man.

Land stupas in the vicinity of the Enlightenment Stupa

Although there may be no direct historical link, my fantasy is that Oddiyana and the stream of realization it represents are very important to this lineage. In fact, even the Sarma schools have an important connection to Oddiyana through such Siddhas as Sarahapa, Nagarjuna, and Luyipa. The Sutra tradition communicated through Buddha Shakyamuni does

Late afternoon light at Vairocana Garden

not thoroughly explain the esoteric teachings first received by King Indrabodhi, which were not written down until many centuries after the time of the historical Buddha. The lineage for those teachings, embodied by such great masters, traces through Oddiyana. It is this that inspired the creation of our modern land of Odiyan.

a place for reflection and contemplation

My Childhood in Golog

Apart from the practical need that our organizations had for a country center, another inspiration for founding Odiyan was my memories of my native land of Golog, in East Tibet (today part of Qinghai Province). Golok is a land of rolling hills and vast prairies, similar in some ways to the rolling hills of Sonoma County, where Odiyan is located. Of course, there is a big difference in elevation. Odiyan is located at 1,400 feet, while Golog is at 14,000 feet.

Like most of the people in Golok, my family lived a nomadic lifestyle, and in the spring and summer months we lived in tents, caring for our herds. As I recall, we lived in encampments of about 40-50 tents, spread out for a distance of perhaps half a mile. This way of life put us in close touch with nature, free to experience the dramatic vistas of our mountain plateau. We lived among the animals we depended on for our livelihood: sheep, horses, yaks, and dzo (female yaks). Each day the herds would be let loose to graze, then brought back at night. Sometimes the herds would cover the land thickly for what seemed like many miles, so that when you looked out from a hill, you could hardly spot any openings.

The vast grasslands in which we camped stretched for miles in all directions, as far as you could see. The only significant trees were small willows, but there were many wildflowers, and at certain times of the year their fragrance would spread everywhere. A small yellow flower with six or seven petals grew close to the river banks, and the flowers in the summer would blanket the ground.

Fragrant Incense Cedars in spring by the reservoir

I remember with great joy the valleys and rivers of my youth. The wild animals in the region, mostly wolves, hawks, and ravens, would prey on the livestock, but they represented little danger to human beings. In the summer when I was a little boy, perhaps three or four, I would often run freely through the fields with other children my age, picking flowers and making up games. One of our games was to bounce echoes off the walls of the valleys. Another was to watch the shapes taking form in the clouds, pushed along by the winds, which could be quite strong. At night, the sky was incredibly clear, and the stars seemed close.

Abundant magnolias bloom in the early spring

Speaking objectively, the climate in Golok could be harsh, with cold winds and snows that sometimes piled up into tall banks. Even today it is not easy to live in such a place, but we were used to it, and we knew how to deal with the challenges.

The dramatic Golok landscape more than made up for these challenges. With so many sudden changes in the weather (especially in the spring and autumn), it was easy to believe that mountain gods and fierce flying dragons were making their presence felt. There were not many sightings of the gods themselves, but we

Magnolias turning toward Vajra Temple

sensed them in the mysterious clouds, the sudden storms, and the dark and looming shapes. It seemed that some mysterious force must be responsible for all the sudden changes, the brilliance of the sun and sky, and the power unleashed in storms. I have heard that nowadays, as global climate change works its effects on my native country, the land is growing more arid, so such dramatic changes may no longer occur.

Even when I was a small child, one aspect of our lives in Golok that troubled me was the way we slaughtered our animals for

Bright yellow ice plant blooming east of the Chapel

food. The Tibetans have historically been big meat-eaters, and the cold and harsh climate, with its short growing season, makes this easy to understand. The only vegetable that grew in the region where I grew up was a kind of small yam, and while it was delicious, it was not really the basis for a vegetarian diet. One of our staples was barley, which we prepared as tsampa, and our yogurt was exceptionally good. Still no one ever questioned the basis of our diet in meat. There were stories of great lamas who had renounced meat-eating for ethical reasons, but these were the rare exceptions.

Vibrant carpet of ice plant in the east Chapel gardens

Of course, as a child, I did not really think about these issues. For me, eating meat was an accepted way of life. What did bother me was to witness the suffering of the animals being slaughtered for us to use. We did not have access to modern techniques, which can be relatively humane, and the animals that I saw being killed were clearly in great pain. I wondered deeply why it had to be that way, and wished that something could be done. Yet I understood very well that we were completely

Thriving Orchids display their

dependent on our animals. Not only did we eat their flesh, but we used every part of their body: the blood, fat, and muscles; the lungs, tongue, heart, and skin. Our clothing, our medicine, and much more came from animals, and their slaughter was unfortunately integral to our way of life. Looking back now, after many years as a vegetarian, I find it remarkable that we all accepted this unthinkingly, when the Buddha teaches as fundamental the commitment to not taking life.

I have returned to Tibet since my departure almost six decades ago, and some elements of the way of life I knew still exist. Mostly, however, they are rapidly changing. The Chinese government has embarked on a long-term program of moving nomads into cities—forcing them into a way of life where they lack even the most basic knowledge of how to survive. The vast open spaces

Looking east from Vajra Temple plaza

still remain, but they are shrinking as more land comes under cultivation and more building and industry develop, while the rivers, which are the lifeblood of the people, are beginning to dry up. When I think of the Tibet of my childhood, with its green trees, vibrant flowers, and happy people, and see how all that is being lost, I can only feel a great sadness.

Many hues of green define midsummer trees and shrubbery

The Foundation for Establishing Odiyan

After receiving an unusually thorough education as a young man, I left Tibet in 1958 to follow my teacher, Jamyang Khyentse Chokyi Lodro. For the next ten years I lived in India, teaching, going on pilgrimage, and starting the publishing projects that would be my main activity for the rest of my life. In 1968, however, I could do more to accomplish my aims by traveling to America. I arrived in New York in 1968, knowing little English and even less about the culture in which I had chosen to immerse myself. I settled in Berkeley a few months later, early in 1969.

In 1971, I founded Padma Ling, an old Berkeley fraternity house near the university campus that we made into a residential center, still operating today. A few years later, I began my search for land for a country center. My childhood home and the heritage of Oddiyana were not uppermost in my mind. Rather, my main concern was to find a permanent home for the Dharma in the West, for I felt that it was my destiny to bring the teachings of the Buddha into the modern world.

It took more than two years, looking at places all over California, but eventually I found the land for Odiyan, on a magnificent site located a hundred miles northwest of Padma Ling. Looking out on the vast Pacific ocean from the crest of Odiyan, the place where we would later build the Central Temple, I found it strange to imagine how a boy from a small village in one of the most remote parts of Tibet had found my way to this new land, so distant, and so different in almost every way.

Emerald Thuja and Japanese maple at home in the Temple gardens

The land that we found more than forty years ago and dedicated forever to the longevity of the Dharma had been home to the Kashaya Pomo Indians for centuries. In the early nineteenth century, the Russians established the first European settlement at Fort Ross, but local ways on the inland ridges remained largely unchanged. In the mid-nineteenth century Mexican and American settlers began entering the coastal lands of Sonoma County. Gradually the land came under the control of private individuals who used it for logging and grazing, and the old way

Orchard fruit trees in bloom

of life, based on hunting and fishing, began to disappear. After several decades of explosive growth as the redwood forests were being logged, the area settled back down into agricultural uses, and the population once more shrank in size.

When we found Odiyan, the land was not in good shape. The trees had been logged for lumber years before, and the land had been grazed and then overgrazed. There were old trees left, the ones that had not been suitable for logging, but many of them were diseased or dying. There were a few spring wildflowers,

Spring in the South Orchard

but everything seemed gray and tired, as though the land itself were exhausted. Tree stumps from the thousands of trees that had been logged were everywhere.

Uprooting those stumps became one of my highest priorities. It took several years, using big machinery. My aim at first was to clear away forty acres that we could use for building temples, but to do that we had to take out thousands of stumps. At the same time, we planted thousands of trees, hedges, and bushes. Eventually we went on to plant grasses and flowers in

an area that took in over a hundred acres. The rest of the land, about a thousand acres in all, was left in its natural state. Gradually, nature itself has helped restore the damage that has been done. We have continued to plant trees and plants; my best estimate is that we have planted over a million trees. Despite the sorry condition of the land, it was clear from the first time I saw it that Odiyan was a magical, unique place. There may not have been dakinis soaring through the skies, but the setting was magnificent: enough to bring joy to anyone who saw it. The vast sky above, completely free of pollution,

Rhododendrons burst forth in Mandala Garden

opens the heart. The majestic ocean in the distance supports wider vision. The winds, which vary from light breezes to howling gusts, remind us of our place in nature. The stars overhead bring to mind the crystal-clear night skies I saw as a child in Golok, and the distinctive seasons give us all the opportunity to explore what it means to be alive.

As I came to know the land in the early days, memories of my childhood returned, and I began to think of the significance of

Spring magnolias surround Vajra Temple

what we were doing in creating a true center for the Dharma in the West. The name 'Odiyan' seemed to me to symbolize perfectly the magnitude of the promise we were making to ourselves, to the lineage, and to future generations.

From the beginning, I determined to do my best to turn Odiyan into a place of beauty, peace, and harmony. This was a way to honor my parents and the land of my childhood, where the simple pleasures that nature provides gave me such

Flowering trees at the Chapel in spring

happiness. I also meant for Odiyan to serve as an offering to the Dharma and a delight to the senses. At the same time, I saw the creation of Odiyan as a gesture of appreciation for the freedom of religion offered by this great country, which had made possible all that I have accomplished during my time in the West. I wanted to give back for all that I have received, and I hoped to build a home for the Dharma here in America that could support and sustain all that is great in this land of boundless blessings.

Early budding magnolias in the North Park

Few of the small group of volunteers who came to build Odiyan in the early days understood much about preserving the land or about construction and design. Most of them had a more intellectual training, and they were unfamiliar with physical labor. Perhaps for that reason, they did not understand why I gave so much effort to beautifying the land, planting trees, bushes, and flowers that came from all parts of the world, reshaping the land with massive earthmoving projects, designating areas as gardens for special cultivation. Funds were short, and our energy limited. We were all volunteers on

One of many red magnolia blossoms at the Chapel

a limited budget, struggling to move forward, working ten to fifteen hours a day with few vacations and only rare days off. Our food was simple and our work hard. We could not afford ordinary comforts that most people took for granted, such as central heating. And there were few opportunities for the usual enjoyments that people in this culture take for granted.

Given these constraints, it was not surprising that volunteers wondered why I devoted so many of our precious resources to the land. Yet I went on planting flowers, bushes, and trees,

Apple tree blossoms in the south Chapel orchard

choosing a wide range of species from all parts of the earth, planning ahead for how Odiyan would look in twenty years, or forty, or even after a century.

For me, the reasons for giving this much energy and attention to the land were never in doubt. In addition to making Odiyan into an offering for the Dharma and a symbol of respect for all the blessings I had received, I hope to bring smiles to the faces of our volunteers and our occasional visitors. In some ways it was a lonely task, because few people really appreciated or

Flowering cherry tree welcomes spring at the Chapel

understood what I was doing. At a purely rational level, I did not understand myself. Still, my intentions were good, and my wish to bring happiness to my students and supporters through the beauty we were creating was real.

Now that Odiyan has become a place of surpassing beauty, I can say that our early sacrifices paid off. Giving our energy and resources to shaping our environment has been a labor of love. Building temples and monuments whose proportions

An early spring on the Temple mound

complement and complete the harmony of the surrounding environment has evoked a sense of fulfillment and completion. Crafting prayer wheels, prayer flags, and stupas in all directions, and working to preserve the tradition, have proved to be a good investment.

Sometimes I myself cannot believe all that we have accomplished. After all, there are few monasteries or even museums that have collections of art equal to ours, and no one has

Maples and evergreens around the Main Temple

produced as many books to distribute to the Sangha. The monuments that grace the Odiyan mandala are symbols of the heart-essence of the teachings we seek to preserve and embody. As for the land of Odiyan, its treasures are now visible to everyone. For those with an open heart, they offer inspiration that naturally turns the mind toward the Dharma.

Today, we see the fruits of our ongoing efforts everywhere we look. The varied greens of the trees and shrubs are a delight. The fragrance of the flowers and the beauty of their blossoms bring new joys and surprises day by day. The environment has

North Park magnolias in early spring

truly been transformed, far beyond what anyone of us could have imagined at the outset. There are big, beautiful parks everywhere, and the ever-increasing presence of animals and birds adds immeasurably to the richness of our experience. The vast ocean, visible so widely from vistas throughout Odiyan, was there long before we came here, but our efforts have created a jewel to ornament that majestic splendor.

We have also benefitted in more immediate ways, for today we rely on Odiyan for much of our food. We have a rich yield each year in apples, walnuts, chestnuts, and figs. Now that we are

Cintamani Temple magnolias

following a vegetarian way of life, the gardens of Odiyan yield a rich bounty. In recent years, we have dedicated more energy to our vegetable gardens, and because residents see the results in their own diets, most people are interested in contributing. Not only are we not supporting the industry that kills animals for food, but we are enjoying more health and experiencing a more wholesome way of life. This seems to me the right way to live—a source of unique blessings.

To me, the choice not to eat meat comes down to a very simple fact: animals have a right to own their own bodies. Even when I was a small boy in Tibet, and I took it for granted that everyone ate meat, it caused me great unhappiness to see

Early in the new year, Daffodils pop open at the Stupa

how the animals suffered when they were butchered—their cries, their eyes rolling up in their heads, the blood pouring to the ground, still warm, and their heart still pumping in the last throes of life. How much better not to be the cause of such pain.

When I first decided to give up meat, I imagined I would miss the taste, but soon I realized that food made from fruits, grains, and vegetables offers more subtle flavors and aromas and richer textures than blood, fat, and meat. Well presented, a vegetarian diet seems to soothe the heart. I cannot imagine that feeding on the blood of other sentient beings promotes healing and inner peace.

Bright daffodils grace Vajra Temple garden

Calling to the Heart

Most of us know how to connect with our senses—seeing, hearing and the rest—at least in a limited way. Often we deliberately seek out new sensations, doing our best to find whatever enjoyment we can. Yet even as we do so, we are cut off from our own hearts, the center of the body and of our inner mandala. Looking here and there for happiness, we no longer know how to comfort our hearts.

Imagine that we could offer our hearts safety, well-being, and security. Imagine that we found ways to restore our heart to its place at the center of the inner mandala, allowing it to circulate healing energies through our whole being. The beauty of Odiyan offers a way for doing just this. Reflecting on the joys that Odiyan offers, I am led to contemplate the inner world of the heart.

O heart, when I visualize you as part of my physical body, I see at once your place in a living, breathing community of organs—the lungs, the liver, the kidneys, the nervous system, and more, and I see how you connect with all my physical being. Yet I never think of you and the tireless work you do. Only when I am in pain or discomfort do I bring you to mind, and then only to complain or worry. Where is my appreciation, dear friend? I have forgotten you.

Perhaps in the past I looked at a textbook image of your workings; perhaps I can even recall the parts that constitute your being: the left and right atrium, the left and right ventricle, tirelessly pumping blood and carrying life-giving oxygen to the

Main temple dome seen through an arbor of cherry blossoms

rest of the body. How intricate the tissues and nerves that run through you; what a wonder their functioning! Yet I never stop to rejoice at this miracle happening at the center of my body in each and every moment—this miracle that you bring about. Now, having brought you to mind, ready to marvel at your workings, I ask with care and gratitude: how do things go with you? You have done so much for me, and in return I have ignored you. Now I wish to end my neglect, and so I ask if all is well. O friend and best supporter, I do care for you. You are a part of me, active at the very center of my mandala of being. Is all well between us? Have you been lonely due to my neglect? Then feel my love, now and from this moment forward.

Spring magnolias reach into the sky near the Chapel

I do not expect you to answer me in words, just as I know that my words will not touch you directly. Yet let them serve as a symbol of my caring and my love. I understand that I can reach you best through the senses, just as you most freely offer me your healing blessings in those moments when the senses come fully alive. And so I have prepared for you a feast of the senses, a richness of beauty. Does the beauty of Odiyan speak to you? Does it reach you, as my words cannot?

You are my living home and my best friend. You are within me, but I am within you as well. Let me offer you security, just as you have given me strength: there is no need to fear

Red magnolias are abundant in late winter at Odiyan

or shut down. Let me offer you recognition: your patient and unending work, which sustains and succors me, will no longer go unnoticed. Let me offer you appreciation, turning from my fascination with the world outside to the treasures within. May you and I rejoin and rejoice, celebrating our eternal bond.

O heart, only thanks to you do my senses offer me beauty and joy. When I see the trees sparkling their greens, it is the blood that you pump through my arteries that makes my seeing

A cozy pair of nesting doves at home in the aviary

possible. When I taste the ripe apple plucked from the tree, I am affirming your vital presence. The sounds that enter my ears, the textures that reveal themselves to my wandering fingers, the raven flapping its wings as it soars across the open field before my eyes, the rhythms of the day as it unfolds through the hours, the rhythms of the seasons as they cycle through the year, bringing me ever new experiences—all these are part of the world you give me.

White dove stays alert on his perch

Heart of my heart, you are also the heart of the world that I discover each day and each moment, through the realm of sense experience you offer me. Appearances play through the field of the senses like marvelous illusions created by master magicians, like artists who join together in dance, spinning intricate patterns out of the dynamic vitality of being alive. Like epic poetry that sings of a time when wonder filled the world, like philosophical musings that open the range of the

The Cherry Mall in full bloom

possible to my questioning mind, like mystic realizations that impress themselves on the most ordinary appearances, the senses bring me home to my own nature, inviting me to celebrate your depths.

O heart, I have long left you alone, ignored and unappreciated, not responding to all that you offer me. Now, however, I freely acknowledge the gifts you have given me. The universe is alive

An offering of blossoms to the Temple

with beauty, with dynamic unfoldings and unique properties that expand far beyond what the intellect can encompass. You are the source for all that I experience, the operator of each new moment. When I enjoy the beauty that surrounds me or marvel at the way life unfolds, I am responding to the blessings you shower upon me. It is through your caring that I can open to my own life. You and I are partners, and it is through your power of manifestation that the world takes shape for me. For such countless opportunities, I thank you.

Rhododendrons add color along Lama's Road

For long I have imagined that I lived alone, responsible for my own affairs, my own understanding, and my own experience. Now I recognized that you have always been there, with me and for me. Best of friends, you steadily offer your support even when I do not recognize your presence. You are my lover, sharing with me the moments I find most precious and the insights that take me beyond the realm of concepts into the rhythmic immediacy of unfolding time. You are my life, filling my senses, my spirit, and my mind with the vital energy of the cosmos.

Cherry blossoms, a delicacy of beauty

I know that I need not sing your praises, and that words will always leave too much unsaid, yet now that I have returned into your presence, I must in some way signal my newly awakened appreciation and joy, My past negligence blinded me, and I forgot the precious resources you made available. Now I know that you are the principal creator, the founder, the cause of my being here, ready to celebrate all that is. I understand at last how much it matters that you are here with me.

Rhododendrons near Vairocana Garden monument

I have grown accustomed to calling myself the owner, the one who knows. I have insisted that 'I am', and I have made of my insistence a truth meant to fill my life with meaning, security and self-importance. Proud of the knowledge I have collected and the abilities I have accumulated over the years, I have tried to build on a foundation that I myself have put in place, never asking whether any sense of security I may experience on this basis can long endure.

Mandala Garden's abundant Rhododendrons

Having chosen not to explore within, where a deeper truth can be found, I have missed my many chances to return to you, my heart. Yet you are the true source of each 'I am' and each 'This is'. Now I understand this, and I see with new eyes. I see that the rhythms of experience match the rhythms you generate. I accept at last that without the light and floating energy you empower, I would have no way to see and hear and feel. Even my limited ways of knowing, my 'thinking about' and the diminished truths I establish, depend on you.

The morning sun highlights magnolias at Vajra Temple

Now that I am attuned to your presence and your magical power, I understand that you are the one who has accommodated my actions and activities, even when I lacked awareness of the role you played. Now I recognize your role, and seeing with such greater clarity, I can project more possibilities and engage the world in more inclusive ways. I can feel my abilities expanding, and I sense that I could participate in your magical way of being. You are the creator, but I can enjoy and benefit from what you make available. Cherishing this realm of boundless availability, I vow to pay

Mature magnolias overwhelm the senses

back your love, your steady commitment, and your boundless willingness to hold open the field of feeling within which I move. O heart, I long to live with you.

My time on earth is limited; that I know for certain. But in the time I have left, may I enter at last the mandala of the body where you reign supreme. I have left much undone, so before I depart, there is much for us to do together. In unity with you, O heart, may my appreciation for all the love you offer steadily grow.

A profusion of yellow iris line the pond

For all these years, I have relied on the heritage transmitted to me by my parents and my teachers and shared with me by my friends and those I love. Their presence illuminates my days, and I know that my love and gratitude for them have not been misplaced. Yet the lineage that sustains me passes through you; for you are the lineage holder. If there is a DNA that codes for meaning, joy, and fulfillment, you are the gene holder. The mandala that radiates out from you is the mandala of my being, in past and present and future. And so I ask: let me find the best way to express my appreciation, through ritual and

A pond of serenity surrounds the Central Mandala

offerings, through worship, through creating delights for the senses and the spirit.

Now at last I know that I am not alone, and knowing this, my kinship with others can be the stable anchor for my actions. With dismay, I see that what I have done, we all have done, again and yet again. We have failed to turn toward you with respect, failed to shape our energies and interactions toward the healing and expansive gestures you inspire. Rather than doing our best to cooperate, we have chosen a path that leads toward disharmony and discord. Not even aware what we were doing, we have allowed head and heart to come into conflict.

Poppies appear "everywhere" near Cintamani Temple

We have treated you poorly, giving little thought to the harm that we are doing, ignoring the damage we do to ourselves.

O heart, you offer us so much, revealing your domain, where gratitude, joy, and happiness all flourish. Yet we turn away. The feel of your presence allows a unique central balance; thanks to you alone we can experience what it is like to be truly present. Yet we choose to go in the opposite direction. Our conceptual mind, centered in the head, creates barriers and erects scarecrows to keep us in line. Its tactic is to lay down rules and set up pros and cons, separating wrong from right and good from bad. Knowing no better, we go along.

California poppies abound at the height of spring

You are not the one to proclaim such divisions, but in our ignorance we impose them, caught in the regime of mind. The head, the chairperson of our privately held corporation, takes over our perception, dictating to us how things are and blinding us to the beautiful, natural presence you hold out unceasingly. Where you are neutral and accepting, the head turns us again and again toward negativity and judgment, discrimination and bias. A whole way of being has been cast in stone, and now we accept its founding pronouncements as true, forgetting what you once revealed.

Trumpet swans enjoy the spring afternoon

O heart, the unhappiness and dissatisfaction that prevail in the world today are not your doing; it is the chief executive of my operating system that decrees how things will be. You brought me jewels, but I tossed them away. You gave me a world flowing with aliveness, dynamic and vibrant, and the ruler of my world froze these gifts into deathly stillness. In a world made rigid and bleak, how can I expect to find joy? A world of delight is available through all the senses, but I have no access. Permission has been denied.

Iris in bloom all along the pond's edge

I know too well this world in which I am trapped. My thoughts and concepts are in control. Like a tyrant in an ancient kingdom, the chairman of my board, who engineered a coup before I knew what was happening has taken over. My options are reduced, and the bitter taste of resentment is on my tongue and fills my nostrils. Everywhere I look, the senses feed back to me the limitations I have taken on as my own—a world of little and less, of doubt and despair. It has all been printed out in advance and handed down to me as law. Day and night I follow the rules that have been promulgated.

Spreading branches intermingle in the Cherry Mall

Spring sun illuminates trees full of flowers

This is not your doing, O my heart. This is not my true being. I have turned my life over to concepts and the intellect, and they have built a prison in which I spend my weary hours. I know how to be skeptical, doubting the possibility for joy toward which you gesture. I know how to be cynical, rejecting any claim that my life could be different. I am quick to spot propaganda and bias, but I do not see how I construct my own positions and insist on them. I follow the lead of the ruler of my regime, all the time, proclaiming myself free. I live in a world where bone-rattling skeletons walk the streets in place of living beings, and I

take my place among them. Yet now I glimpse the truth of what is so, for I sense that you are here to show another way.

How does it stand with me? Mostly I do not realize what I have done; I fail to understand how turning from your blessings destroys what is best in my own life. Proud and arrogant, inwardly satisfied with the fruits of my own radical destructiveness. I call the way of life to which I have submitted the path of intelligence and clear-sightedness. Walking this path, I know how to be critical of myself and others, but not how to turn toward what is positive and healing. Having lost my connection with you, O heart, I suffer the consequences.

Fragrant rose beds line the inner Stupa garden

If I knew how to acknowledge you and nourish your inner goodness, so that you in turn could nourish me, I could still turn things around. But that is not the path I have chosen. Instead, I keep my thoughts and perceptions secret, even from myself, hoarding them in fear and suspicion. I do not feed you whatever good things I experience—the beauty and pleasure, the positive and the meaningful. Instead, I keep them for myself. Doing so, I choke the life out, I consign them to oblivion. Instead of healing beauty, I send you only toxic signals. I force them through my nervous system, where they congeal and fester and cannot flow. I am trapped in my own bias and resentment, and that is all I have to offer you.

Miniature roses at the Stupa

O heart, having turned from you, I embody the limited, deadly serious truths of the conceptual world I have learned to call home. Harsh dictators issue decrees, and I must obey. The luminous net of realization that lights up the world has been transformed into a net of thoughts that catch me up, leaving me tangled in my own confusion, lost and secretly crying tears I am too numb to notice.

I know too well how it is to live this way. Countless names describe the patterns of my days. There is the resentment

Luminous purple iris along the Stupa road

that makes me turn from what is positive as though it posed a threat. There are the bad memories from which I hide, but which loom up in the dark moments of the night. There are the scarcely noticed moments of defeat and acquiescence that line my prison walls. There is the paranoia that makes me afraid to venture out into the world, fearing it will feed me back my own negativity. I call myself insensitive; I call myself uncomfortable; I call myself uneasy; I call myself a failure. In place of joy and peace, I know only loneliness and countless forms of inner toxicity. Rather than float in your realm of joy

Iris displays majestic color at the Chapel

joy and appreciation, I feed back to you this ghastly mix of poisons. I concoct out of my own negativity a venomous stew, forcing you to taste what I myself can hardly bear.

O heart, I know full well that all joy lies in returning home to live in your realm of fullness and peace, yet I let myself be pulled away again and again. Drifting aimless, cut off from your nourishment, I tell myself there is somewhere else I can be, something else I can do, some unknown someone who holds the key to my well-being. Wanting something else, I am disloyal to you. I abandon you, and feel abandoned in turn.

A cluster of Stupa roses

I have treated you wrongly. But now, seeing what I have done, I am ready to come back to you, to be your friend, to open to my own nature and relax in the embrace of your love. I have been a slave to my own confusion and desire, my own misunderstanding, but now I will seek true comfort and ease. I know now that my head must yield its usurped place of power, approaching you in peace, ready to cooperate. I do not need to accept the 'truths' my thoughts and concepts present; I do not need to feel the feelings they insist are real. I do not need to follow out the whole sad story I have called my life.

Brilliance before the Prayer Wheels

O heart, I have wandered far away. Now I need to retrace my steps. Give me the key, so that I can once more gain entrance your realm. I know already how to care for my body and worry about its health; now it is time to care for the heart. As long as I live, let me dwell in your presence. I want to meet you, to be with you, to unite with you.

Perhaps it is too much to ask for union, at least for now. At least, then, help me pause for a moment in my frantic pursuit of negativity and inevitable frustration. Let me simply

Roses bloom for months on the Temple mound

come into your presence, so that we can greet one another as friends. Even if it happens only once, may my connection with you grow, opening the door to a new way of being.

I have certainly had moments of joy and positivity in the past, and now I realize that in those moments you and I were in communication. Perhaps I sensed that I could connect with my own feelings in a different way, that I could open to you; that I need not go through my life actively ignoring what I was feeling. Yet the old drama played itself out again and again,

A red bouquet in the Stupa courtyard

its force too strong for me to resist. In the next moment I was once again kidnaped, led back to my cell and put back under the custody of my captors: language, images, and social pressures. Unable to trust my own experience, I was overcome with shame, embarrassment, and shyness. Looking back, it seems I had little choice. The freedom I thought was mine was an illusion. And so I once again abandoned you, my own sweet heart. Doing so, I abandoned myself.

A rose for the heart's goodness

And yet, and still, I dare to ask you now, O heart, on behalf of myself and all those I care for—my parents, my best friends, and all who depend on me—let me return to you. I can at least communicate clearly what I need, if you are willing to listen. Let me draw near, let me touch you, if only now and then. This is a new thought for me, so I speak with hesitation. This is not how I have learned to think; this is not how I have learned to act, but still I am ready to try. Is it possible that we could once again cooperate? Will you grant me a second chance?

A rose to bring good cheer

For so long, I did not understand who was the operator of my being. Now I know—you are the source for my presence and my life. How could I not have seen this before? How could it be that you were hiding in plain view?

Perhaps it was that my usual ways of looking and labeling could not guide me. I could not look beyond the physical and the objective; I had no deep knowledge of how you came to inhabit my being. Where did your energy manifest; how did it manifest? How did you perform your magic? I could not truly

Late summer "naked ladies" at Vairocana Garden

see your size and shape and color, and so I missed the many indications of your presence. You spoke to me in the rhythm of the senses, like a secret, sacred music I could not allow myself to hear. Acting on a level too crude, too polluted, I poisoned you in my ignorance, so that you could not flow sweetly and gently, could not pump through the systems of my body and spirit the vital energy that nourished my soul.

Always in your presence, I was sensitive only to the signals I myself originated, signals that spoke of resentment and

Lilies on the grassy hill near the Chapel

discomfort. Entangled in countless toxic residues, frozen into the fixed structures that the regime of mind put in place, I was blind. You sent me nectar; I sent it back congealed and tainted. Caught in my disorders, I blocked the healing flow you sought to make available.

Now I wish to change all that. Here at Odiyan, in this realm of sacred beauty, I am ready to nourish you, so that you may nourish me. Let me share with you the power and blessings of the natural world, the splendor of these gardens, the lovely

An island of flowers upon entering Vairocana Garden

delicacy of the flowers, the vigorous energies of the animals that make their way in the world without little concern for their human fellow travelers. Let us drink in together, the intimate engagements of the birds and waterfowl, the endless openness of the sky, and the awe-inspiring vastness of the night.

Knowing full well that these are not mine to give, I dare to offer them—this magical display, these aesthetic rhythms. Accept what has always been yours, so that the energies you make available can once more flow freely. I honor you as the source

Sunny greenery at Vairocana Garden

for my being alive today. Please embrace these outer tokens of your inner beauty as agents of my caring. As for me, I freely acknowledge your presence at the center of my being.

I know full well that there are higher realms of being and further realms of sacred knowledge, and I proclaim my wish to enter into union with such dimensions, so that I can offer you the realization they bring. Yet for now, I offer what I can: whatever I know or see; whatever beauty I encounter. Whatever insights my own limited understanding can accommodate, I

Clematis blooms in the Chapel gardens

send to you and share with you. The beauty that inspires me and flows through the daily events of my life, I will offer you. That is my commitment to you, now and always. Any taste or texture, every joy, every positive quality—the nectar of life itself—I give to you, knowing that you are their source; that I am paying back to you what you have made available.

The natural beauty of Odiyan I have done my best to emulate in my work here. That is the secret meaning of this mandala, with its monuments and temples, built to harmonize with

Princess flower blossoms in Vairocana Garden

nature and complete its promise. May the blessings that Odiyan evokes radiate outward, touching all beings whose hearts are attuned to inner peace. I cannot say whether the animals and birds of Odiyan realize in their own being such heartfelt truths, but I know that human beings have such power, for we are free. In the name of that freedom, may we feed back to you all the bountiful opportunities we are given. May all beings act in goodness; may they be healthy and happy, and may they be loyal to their own hearts and to the promise of perfect realization. To make this possible is my mission, and I dedicate the fruits to you.

A cluster of multi-colored tulips and hyacinth

O heart, I offer my thanks for whatever I have been able to enjoy in my life, so often without regard for you. Filled with gratitude and wonder, I acknowledge your kindness in sharing such blessings. You have revealed to me this world as magical, and through the inner peace you offer, I have learned what it means to live in a magical kingdom of delight and meaning.

With your blessing, I can purify the toxic waste that pollutes the river of my life, the poison that has caused you so much pain. No longer willing to neglect your needs, I can learn to

Trees of colorful, fragrant roses border the lawns

see the world through your eyes. No longer inhabiting a world bounded by the distinctions between subject and object, pro and con, good and bad, I can recognize appearance in all its manifestations as a source of bountiful blessings. And perhaps through learning to live this way, I can also help to heal the outer environment, for I understand now that the inner and outer environments share with one another all that matters most.

Parrot tulips brighten the Main Temple maple beds

For so long, my heart, you have had no spokesman, no protector—all due to my neglect. The henchmen of the chairman, the ruler of the regime, slipped in and kidnapped you at knife point, conspiring with concepts and the intellect, urged on by those who proclaim themselves searchers and seekers. Now, that conspiracy has been exposed. You are restored to your rightful place at the center of my being, and I celebrate your return to the throne.

A variety of tulip blossoms mark the onset of spring

Long ago, your captors seized control. They tried in vain to fix the ills that beset the world. For decades, even centuries, they sought to demonstrate that they could put an end to suffering, yet all their plans and schemes proved to be of no avail. How sad to see the wasted effort, the false beginnings, the discouraged and disillusioned endings. Freed from the power of self-deception and the false views of those who have so long been in charge, I can recognize in sorrow the harm that has been caused.

First rose of spring in the Main Temple gardens

Now, O heart, you are once again in power, and I see the possibilities for freedom and fulfillment bright before my eyes. And so I ask you, send your healing energy out into the world, so that all may benefit. Fill me with your blessings, so that the difficulties I have known and the sorrows that plague all sentient beings can be healed and transformed. Let me discover for myself the joys that life has to offer, so that I can pass this message, this good news, on to others. In return, I pledge to care for you, to treat you with love, devotion, and respect.

Rhododendrons among the stupas in Mandala Garden

The opportunity we all share as human beings is so rare, so precious. Every minute, every hour, every day is a priceless jewel. Now that you are once more at the center of my being, I pledge to act with full commitment. What we have can be lost if we do not act; we see it happening everywhere. I pledge to act to prevent such waste.

My heart, I see around me pain and sorrow. More than 7 billion people live on this earth, each trying for happiness and well-being. They fight with each other, they struggle to secure

Summer snowflake viburnum on Temple lawn

their futures, they do what they can to improve their fortunes. They protect what is theirs, and they enter into schemes to grow richer or more powerful, to free themselves from the rule of others, to safeguard their loved ones and their belongings from all sorts of external dangers. Yet within, it seems their hearts are bleeding. Show me, O heart, how to help them. Let them learn to appreciate their own inner environment. Let them find ways to put an end to the patterns of neglect they have learned from childhood onward.

Pale viola miraculously appears in the Temple garden

I see now with ever increasing clarity how good intentions and ideas are not enough. The efforts human beings make fall short, or head off in directions leading only to more danger and more suffering. We know how to travel to Mars or other planets, but we do not know how to turn inward, asking our hearts what they need. We ignore what we know to be true. We fail to be loyal to ourselves, and so the path to inner peace and freedom—the road home—is blocked.

A newborn mini catches his balance on jittery legs

O heart, we all know this to be true, and yet we know no other way. Science offers marvelous technologies, amazing for one like me, who was raised in a very different world. Yet each new solution to the ills that limit our lives brings forth new problems, sometimes worse than the old. We seek power over others, but cannot gain power over our own minds. We build up riches, but find we cannot buy at any price what we most wish for. Our attempts to be the ones in charge breed resentment and foster resistance. The security we seek is beyond us; the answers we require elude us.

A baby Kiger Mustang rears up in the morning sunlight

Yet it is not too late. Our lives may be passing, but we can use the time left to us to develop more understanding and greater appreciation. In every second, always starting over, we can let the joy and harmony we know already be our guide to a different way of life. We can open the senses and heal the mind. Acting on what we know in our heart of hearts, when it is time for us to leave this world, we will have no regrets. We will be ready to take our leave nicely, gently, with words of thanks on our lips and in our hearts.

Oriental Lilies open their petals wide

This world that we have created, O heart, the world we see when we look around us, is a world from which you have been banished—kidnapped, locked away, We could free you—we have that power. But we do not have the key, not because it is held by others, but because we do not know how to ask for it, do not know how to win your trust. We tell ourselves we are smart, smarter than those who have come before, able to do more than any people in history. But we are not smart enough to know how to restore communication with our hearts.

Blooming Oriental Lily in Vairocana Garden

Help us see clearly this world we have created, where little is genuine, where everything has been determined in advance, where openness to new energies and new understanding are in short supply. How sad to live in a world where we only know how to make our way conceptually, based on our plans, the structures we establish, and the labels we assign. How wasteful to inhabit an artificial world, a virtual-reality world, showy, but with no depth—a cartoon of a world, in which we become cartoon versions of ourselves.

Glow of evening sky over

Here we stand, trying to take our place in the world we have brought into being. But we have doomed our efforts before we begin. We may have built the best search engines, but we only know how to search in certain limited dimensions and domains. We know how to poke and point, how to criticize and undermine. We know the way of the cynic and the skeptic, but we do not know how to open to ourselves to our own hearts, how to contact the heart. And when the heart does speak, we are not ready to trust it, for we hear it only as another voice, perhaps another demand. We are so used to

the Chapel grounds

being divisive that we cannot hear the still, small voice that offers healing and peace.

Can we find a new search engine, one that leads us into the pathways of the heart? Can we learn to feel our way into the essence of our own being? We will need to develop trust and genuine knowledge. Yet when I take your counsel, O heart, I find new confidence that a single step in that direction may be enough, for you impart to me the vital truth that trust builds on trust and knowledge builds on knowledge.

Bright red, orange and yellow leaves of Liquid Amber

The old ways of knowing—the ones that turn from you, O heart—depend on separation and distinctions, on labels that cover up rather than revealing. We speak of space, that realm of openness, and since we look first to our labels, we imagine we are referring only to emptiness, or to the distant, empty sky, remote and far removed from our concerns. Yet when we ask with our hearts, ask with more concern for our own being, we see that space makes possible appearance—appreciating space, we discover a gateway to the realm of the heart.

Rays of sunlight through the groves of trees

After all, what does it mean to occupy space? What has become of the ones who occupied space in the past—say 240 years ago, when this country was founded? What is the nature of the space that they occupied? When they left, what did they leave behind? Not all beings occupy space in the same way: can we appreciate multiple ways of occupying? What did it mean to occupy space five billion years ago, and what will it mean to take shape and form in space twenty billion years from now? These question seem remote to the conceptual mind, but they are questions for the heart. Can knowing with the heart lead us into the heart of such questions?

Flowering Acacia in late winter near the Chapel

To find new pathways of knowledge, we will need to ask new questions. We will need agents who are not simply robots of our desire, robots ready to create fictions and constructs, solutions and technologies, but lacking knowledge of the pathways that lead to the realm of the heart. Only by proceeding sensitively, O heart, can we invite your presence; only then can we open to you. Here at Odiyan, I see clearly, and proclaim for all to hear: we must let the old structures and the old ways of knowing melt away, so that the streams of nectar, of universal caring free from bias, can once more flow through our lives.

Early signs of spring at the Chapel

In Touch with Nature

What is it about nature that can be so healing, that justifies the resources we have spent to bring more beauty to the Odiyan land? In one way the answer is obvious. All of us, residents, volunteers, and visitors can enjoy the colors and textures and fragrances of the plants and trees and bushes and the soaring elegance of the birds flying overhead. The beauty of nature smiles at us: it communicates to our hearts and inspires our senses. It turns us toward appreciation and love, and toward the simple joys we experienced as children.

All cultures understand this at some level. The Western Bible has the story of the Garden of Eden. It is good to reflect on what life would have been like for Adam and Eve before the fall, when they wandered without care in the natural world.

The Buddhist tradition has similar accounts of the Pure Lands, and especially Amitabha's Pure Land, known as Sukhavati. It is a world of floating palaces, of lotus ponds and elegant gardens, where all basic needs are fulfilled and the air is rich with wonderful fragrances and beautiful sounds that turn the mind toward the Dharma.

Such descriptions remind us that when the senses enjoy fulfillment, we are satisfied within, and we easily find inspiration to act on our highest values. Deeply connected to the world we inhabit, we realize we are part of nature. We rejoice in its silent beauty, its rich colors, and the rhythms of change that communicate in accord with their own dynamic the truth of natural harmony.

Towering trees around Anandabhadra Library

The beauty we experience through the senses supports the practice of meditation, which opens inner realms of beauty and peace. Today, however, this simple truth is not easy to recognize. We are so busy, so caught up in our own thoughts and projects, that we cannot appreciate the world we inhabit. Often when we visit places of great beauty, we drive through them instead of taking the time to savor what they offer us. We do not have the time to see, to enjoy, to contact. It is natural to appreciate and enjoy, but for us, in our hurried and worried

Shrubs at Vairocana Garden in bloom

state, we may need special training or special opportunities to connect our soul and senses with peacefulness, joy, and an artistic creativity. Instead, we too often learn to think of nature as something to use and abuse, to bend to our will, even if it means destroying it in the process. The beauty of Odiyan can serve as an antidote to these ways of being.

Most people are far removed from a deep connection with nature, because they have few opportunities to be in nature on

Dogwoods flower in the North Park by mid-spring

a regular basis. After all, most of us live in cities. City parks are better than no nature at all, but often they are somewhat unnatural, carefully manicured, or designed around showy and artificial features. How much better if we can walk in gardens, stroll through valleys, look out over inspiring vistas, or sit at the side of lakes. We can enjoy the air, the sunlight, the breezes, the smells. Many people today often feel isolated and alone, but if we can connect with nature, it is like greeting a good friend, a valued partner whose very presence nourishes you.

Odiyan's view of the Pacific extends from

Many Americans I meet have a love affair with music. They are always listening to music, no matter what else is going on. Of course, there are many needs that music may fill, but nature can do so just as well. The same is true for the arts: beauty, painting, architecture. At Odiyan we celebrate the beauty of art for its power to connect us with the sacred, but we should not forget that nature has similar charms. It shows us shapes and forms that are naturally pleasing, forms whose qualities, impressions, and expressions are uplifting and transformative.

the southeast to the western horizon

Communing with nature can be like falling in love. In touch with nature, we need have no concerns, for the benefits of nature are always available and sure to bring joy. When we confine our love to other human beings, there is always the risk that circumstances and conditions may change. We may fall out of love, or they may, or we may lose them unexpectedly. Sometimes such relationships will lead to great happiness, sometimes the opposite. With nature, we can coordinate the rhythms of our experience, whatever they may be. We can invite in the heart, and mind, the soul and the senses, This is an opportunity we cannot afford to ignore.

For me, the name Oddiyana evokes these possibilities. Once upon a time, Oddiyana was a land of power, a mystical land

Amitayus Ridge in the late afternoon

that transmitted the spiritual dimension of our being into the world we inhabit. Today we may not be able to touch this same dimension easily, but the Odiyan we know and have helped create can give us a comparable opportunity to engage the nature of beauty and meaning directly. Our world today, beset by so many problems—pollution that fouls the air and water and disturbs the mind—is in great need of such an immediate and direct teaching. We are on the verge of losing something of great value, and Odiyan can help restore it. At Odiyan, the rhythms of our mind can connect with the rhythms of nature. The impressions and expressions that shape Odiyan's environment can call us back to ways of living that we are in danger of forgetting.

View to the northwest from Vajra Temple

Learning from Odiyan

Odiyan is like a vast book that we can read and enjoy, almost like a Bible or other sacred text that reveals to us truths important to know. Of course, Odiyan does not speak to us in words, but it does offer a rich treasury of knowledge for the senses. At a deep level, it reveals to us the bounty that time and space offer and shows us how our own lives fit into the rhythms of nature.

Think of your life up to this moment in time. We all have memories of childhood, whether positive or negative, but much of our lives has simply disappeared from memory; as far as we can tell, it has had no impact on our present experience. Do we know how we arrived here, or have we forgotten? How much can we trace out? Looking back, we may not notice changes as they arise, day by day and week by week. One day, however, we will awake to the consequences. Our bodies are aging: our hair disappearing, our bones growing more brittle, muscle strength melting away. Acknowledging this, we can remind ourselves to take the opportunities life presents before they are lost.

Nature is a more subtle teacher. It invites us appreciate what is happening from moment to moment, present to present. Wherever we go, whatever activities we undertake, we can attune ourselves to the rhythms of nature, which unfold beyond our power to control. Nature reminds us that we should never dismiss the values of beauty. The path through which our lives take shape offers important opportunities, and nature asks us to notice and appreciate what is happening. It offers impressions and expressions that can lead us toward truth.

A profusion of roses at Vairocana Garden

The rhythms of nature teach us how events unfold and encourage us to accept whatever happens. Just as some days will be sunny and others stormy, there may be times when our positive feelings give way to sadness or pain, disappointment or disillusionment. Yet those unfolding rhythms do not shape or define us. If we accept them for what they are and seize the truth that they contain, we quickly discover that they are marked by endless transitions. At Odiyan, the winter rains and cold can be difficult, but we know that the spring and summer will return, bringing beauty so powerful it exceeds our memories and our expectations.

Mature Tan Oak in east orchard

Once we recognize the rhythms of time at work in our own lives, difficult situations will not undermine our ability to enjoy what life presents. We will not be tempted to blame ourselves when things go wrong or people react negatively to something we have done or said. When we condemn ourselves or judge ourselves harshly, or when we decide that we are failures, we are responding to a situation that will change—quickly or over time—as surely as the seasons of our lives give way, one to the next. Recognizing that our attempts to hold on or push back only set us up for unhappiness, we will be able to see the situation more honestly and accurately.

Robinia pseudoacacia frisia, golden from early spring

Perhaps we do have stormy thoughts and feelings, but we can simply accept that. Perhaps we do feel lonely and insecure, but that is not the final, ultimate truth of the matter. We need to say, "Yes, I have been like this; I have reacted in this way. Now I will do it differently; I know that I can. It is time to move on, to let the rhythms of time unfold, accepting their momentum."

To encourage this kind of reaction, it helps to relax the breath and let the mind grow clean, clear, and calm. Then we discover our own inner aliveness and the opportunity it offers. Our life is not some barren desert, but a living field rich in the

potential for growth. We can plant more seeds of goodness and cultivate the shoots. We can water our intentions with good thoughts, kind thoughts that gently release the visionary way we have chosen to embody. Every day, every hour, we can develop appreciation for our own possibilities, connecting to our potential. Just as the Odiyan community needs to connect with the land, the temples, and the mandala, so we all need to connect internally with our body, mind, spirit, and faculties, and even with our fundamental energies, right down to the chemical interactions happening within each cell.

Spring color in the Mandala Garden

If we want to make sure a plant will grow well and blossom into beauty, it is our responsibility to nourish and care for it. In the same way, we should treat ourselves with respect, not encouraging inner conflict or bias. We have had enough bias, enough discrimination, and enough condemnation. We have put up with enough delusions, enough poisons, enough insecurity, enough loneliness. Really: enough!

Now is the time. We can create a rich and healthy environment for growth. Like the natural world in which we live and breathe, we are dynamic and vital creatures. We are not the

last survivors of a dying race, gasping out our final breaths in a desert too parched to sustain life. We are alive, and we can support growth and beauty from within.

We can also share the potential we find in ourselves with others. I have been told that trees in the forest communicate with each other, and that when one is unhealthy, the others send it nourishment and share their resources through their roots. That is how we can be with others. We can share what we have discovered, in part through what we say, but also

Daisies at Vairocana Garden

through what we do and how we manifest. In a sense, that is our duty, our mission. We know we are not perfect, but we have something to offer. Whatever we find in ourselves that is rich and wholesome, healthy and beautiful, we can make available to others, even in our simplest actions. In that way, knowledge will deepen and expand. Eventually it can become infinite, like jewels whose inner depths go on forever.

Roses in the Stupa garden

Often at Odiyan I have noticed the different kinds of trees. Some stay green throughout the year; some lose their leaves and stand naked during the winter, but are reborn each spring. Others, like the magnolias, change color in the autumn, bringing fresh new delight. Many trees and bushes flower each year, displaying intense beauty for weeks at a time.

Stupa garden Penstemon

Our own nature is similar. There are countless ways in which we can express our own inner worth, qualities in ourselves—and in others—that we have forgotten to appreciate. Our own ability to love and feel joy, to be free and alive, to discover an inner youthfulness: these are all available, and by touching them we can inspire ourselves to touch more deeply our own capacities.

Each of us has a beautiful inner garden. Perhaps we only find ourselves there from time to time, in moments when there are

Azaleas near the Chapel

no distractions and conflicts or problems, moments when we feel light and free and are transported to a place of peace and harmony. Such moments come and go, so we need to learn to take advantage of the opportunities they offer without trying to hold on to them. Like nature, the body and mind have their own rhythms, and it is best to let them unfold in accord with their inner dynamic. Then we will discover that we can effortlessly cultivate in ourselves the virtuous qualities we value most—love, joy, compassion, balance, and wisdom. Our mind, and also our spirit, are capable of this. We can embody

Lilacs in the Chapel gardens

such qualities, so that other people recognize them as well, sharing the benefit such treasures bring. In this way, our heart and soul will stay vital and alive, and we will leave the desert of loneliness and despair far behind.

As human beings living in the realm of desire, we have known our fill of delusion and illusions, controversy and conflict. Yet that is not the truth of our being. There are treasures within each of us that manifest Dharma transmission and perfect wisdom. We can connect with them 'animisticly' through our soul. We should not make our own nature into an enemy, The

natural world teaches us that goodness and beauty are ever available, and that is true for our own nature as well.

Most of us can say with confidence that when we were born, our parents welcomed us with love and joy, and that they nurtured our growth into adulthood, wishing for us that we be happy. Our friends and those we love share that wish. The Christian tradition would add that God loves us and wants our happiness, and in Buddhism we would say the same of the Buddha and the Great Bodhisattvas. We can have that same wish for ourselves, and we can expand it out to all beings.

Late afternoon view of Vajra Temple from the west rim

Without sentient beings to guide toward enlightenment, Bodhisattvas would have no job. What about us? What is our job, our reason for being on earth? In one way or another, isn't it our responsibility to cultivate kindness toward all beings, to act with love and thoughtfulness, aiming always to promote joy? Those with greater understanding always seek our happiness. In the same way, we can share with others whatever knowledge and wisdom we discover and embody.

Flowering cherry tree in full bloom at the Chapel

The beauty of nature as it manifests here at Odiyan can help us discover such knowledge. When we cultivate a deeper seeing, a rich experiencing, Odiyan can open vastly the truth of our experience, chapter by chapter and petal by petal. We can embody more fully what we come to understand, letting kindness and joy spread through our being. When we are completely open, beauty will unite with wisdom, and wisdom will unite with compassion. There will be no room for guilt, fear, and misunderstanding.

A plum tree encloses Avalokiteshvara at Cintamani Temple

Each of us can take responsibility for our own spiritual path. We can choose not to go in a wrong direction. Here, reading books, attending classes and seminars, or accumulating degrees that demonstrate our knowledge can be helpful, but the knowledge that will truly benefit us is the knowledge we learn through living our lives. Our own experience can teach us the insights that will transform our way of being.

Nobody needs to tell us what to do, what steps to take. The beauty of what is already available can guide us. We can bring

South entryway with flowering plum trees

out our own potential—we can secure it, encourage it, and make sure from day to day and moment to moment that we do not lose it. Now is the time to embark on that path.

We can be our own partner, relishing the feel of our own existence, caring for our own embodiment. The world today is caught up in bias and enemy-making on the one hand and distraction on the other. But we can choose not to be part of these patterns—the impressions that are constantly being put forward and the expressions that are steadily being broadcast.

Dutch iris near the Vajra Temple monument

We do not have to participate in the violent destruction of what has value.

All of us do have moments of enjoyment, but most of the time we let our sense of burdens and problems overwhelm us. Work is a burden, being busy is a burden, obligations are a burden, society's demands are a burden, people's expectations are a burden. Because I have so many burdens, I cannot fully respond, so then I feel guilty, and now my guilt is a burden. If I procrastinate, there is just more guilt. If I make

Central Temple dome rises above cherry blossoms

excuses, maintaining the structure that supports my excuses is a burden. As the English expression puts it, we are caught between a rock and a hard place. We know how to label our situation, we know how to make judgments about what is good and what is bad, but we do not know how find lasting joy.

Imagine your parents were standing before you today. Gazing at you with love, they might say what parents almost always say: "Enjoy yourself. Do what makes you happy." Are we following that wise counsel, or are we letting ourselves be

The glory of spring blooms in the Cherry Mall

overwhelmed by negativity, by the problems we see rising up on all sides? Of course, we also wish for our own happiness, but do we let ourselves feel the appreciation that makes true happiness possible?

Who is the navigator plotting the course our life is taking? Do we even have a clue? Are the answers we give trustworthy? If we look closely, it seems we do not know. Yet that knowledge is available. It manifests in our hearts and minds when we

learn to experience joy and wonder, appreciation and care. As we begin to explore these dimensions of our being, preparing well for the next moment of our lives, we can act to fulfill our purpose in being born into this world

We can also share with others the knowledge we are learning to embody. When we are partners with ourselves, we can make our life into a beautiful work of art that we can enjoy and present to others. We can communicate the positive qualities we manifest.

Red rhododendron

Many people today emphasize staying in touch with the body, but that advice will not help much if we do not understand what the body is showing us. The body is not there to support our endless cycles of guilt and worry, our repetitive thoughts and plans and concerns. We think it is wise to plan things out and to act on our concerns. We tell ourselves that if we know how to worry, we will also know how to make ourselves

An Iris catches the morning sunshine

secure. But all that makes sense only as long as we base our lives on grasping. It all looks very different if we ground ourselves in appreciation; if we acknowledge the beauty around us and the efforts that others have made to secure our well-being. This is what matters about our embodiment; it is the reason we are here. These are lessons that Odiyan can teach us.

Clematis vines bloom near the Chapel gate

Sharing the Blessings

Our work for the Dharma expresses our wish to ensure its longevity in these rapidly changing times. The teachings of the Buddha have their roots in the East, but now we are helping put down new roots in the West. We do not want the wisdom of the Dharma to disappear, so we support the sacred languages of the Dharma and the symbols through which the Dharma takes form in the world. It has been our great good fortune to restore and transmit these blessings. My wish is that our community continues to do so for a long time to come.

Sometimes visitors come to Odiyan to participate in what we have created here. Delegations of Vietnamese Buddhists have been here, and teachers representing other traditions have joined us as well. We are grateful for their faith and appreciation, which encourages us to do more. When visitors join us from other parts of the world, worshipping at the Stupa or at our temples, or simply appreciating the beauty of Odiyan, we rejoice. Their joy at being here affirms that we have been able to communicate something of the value of the Dharma and the blessings it brings. Sharing these blessings is a powerful support for our own practice.

Odiyan is also my present to those who live here and have lived here, in the past, present, and future, including those who have passed on. I hope that everyone living at Odiyan now and in the future finds opportunities to appreciate and enjoy the splendors of Odiyan and let its healing power enter your body, spirit, and mind. I hope also that you will do your part to

Italian cypress encircle the Stupa

maintain Odiyan for the benefit of those yet to come. When we arrived at Odiyan, the land was chaotic and disturbed. Now it is rich in shape and form and beauty, in qualities that all of us can appreciate. One sign of this transformation is the growth in animal life, which today is rich and varied.

Maintaining this beauty will require continuing vigilance. We all know that globally the climate is changing, and I am concerned that we preserve our limited Odiyan water supply and use it well. I have drilled many new wells over the years, some successful and some not, and we have installed

Petunias in bloom at Vairocana Garden

many solar panels. Perhaps in the future we will be able to find other ways to take full advantage of our resources and develop new ones.

Like the early Odiyan volunteers, who were focused on building projects and tended not to appreciate the beauty of the environment, Tibetans who look at Odiyan from a distance have sometimes questioned why we have devoted so many resources to making Odiyan a place of beauty. Why not take the money that goes into Odiyan and put it to other uses, they ask. After all, there are many humanitarian

Miniature roses adorn Vairocana Garden

projects intended to benefit the Tibetan people that are in need of financial assistance.

One answer to that question is that we have indeed offered support for such projects. We have donated to schools and medical clinics and to create water systems that can provide safe water supplies. Beyond that, of course, I have done as much as I could to preserve Tibetan culture and its Dharma heritage. Our projects have had a significant influence in India, Nepal, Bhutan, and Tibet, and even in China and Southeast

A field of Dutch white clover near Cintamani gate

Asia. Our work to preserve sacred art and to restore the holy places of the Buddha is ongoing, and I hope that untold numbers of beings share in the blessings that result.

Yet I feel no need to defend the choices we have made. I truly believe that in the future, the mandala of Odiyan will be a place that brings great benefits to all beings. Residents and visitors alike will be able to enjoy its offerings for the senses, and through their enjoyment they will learn what it means to appreciate and care for themselves and for others, and also for

Sunflowers in the vegetable garden

this wonderful planet we inhabit. For those who make Odiyan their home, those lessons mature over time. Even those who come here only for a short stay, however, can join us in caring for what has been created and preserving its special power. For all who walk this land, let your senses and your hands be gateways to your soul. Let yourself feel what Odiyan offers, and be open to what the mandala communicates. Let Odiyan truly become a part of your life.

The reservoir provides life-sustaining water to much of Odiyan's

I have produced this book as a support for what Odiyan offers. It celebrates and records the beauty that manifests here. Perhaps it will help you appreciate more deeply the beauty of the environment and the power of the mandala. It may also remind you to be grateful to America for the freedom it offers, which has made it possible to create this enchanted realm, and to the State of California and the County of Sonoma for safeguarding the natural splendor of this part of the world.

plantlife; the ever-present Pacific breezes keep prayer flags aloft

Toward the Future

We have been at Odiyan for more than forty years, steadily working to make it into a Dharma realm. Most companies and businesses in America do not survive that long, so I am proud of what we have been able to accomplish. Few people have much understanding of the cost and complexity of building Odiyan and maintaining it over the years, but many people have helped make Odiyan a reality. It has been a big task, made possible only through the cooperation and loyalty of my friends, my family, my students, and my supporters, who mostly have been ready to accept my guidance.

For myself, I am now in my 82nd year. I do not understand the meaning of retirement, so I continue to work for the Dharma and for the sake of those who have given me so much. Reflecting on my five decades in this land, the ten years I spent in India, and my years of study and training in Tibet, I am naturally led to reflect on my childhood in Tibet and on my parents, for that is where this journey began.

My father passed away soon after the communists seized control in Tibet in 1959, but my mother survived, a fact I did not learn for more than thirty years after leaving Golok. Luckily, I was able to visit her on three separate occasions before she passed away. The stories she told me of the worst years of Chinese rule were difficult to hear. My family was wealthy by the standards of my region, the Sogpo clan to which we belonged was respected, and my father was well known as a Dharma teacher, village leader, healer, astrologer, and Pobdag (responsible for guiding the dead to rebirth in a

View of Cintamani Temple from the road to the reservoir

higher realm). Accordingly, the local Chinese officials were very hard on my family, whom they condemned as feudal lords. Morning to evening, several days a week, they subjected my mother and others in my family to re-education sessions. My aunt, a famous beauty and the mother of several prominent lamas, was forced to stand barefoot on the frozen river ice for hours at a time while officials shouted out indoctrination.

Villagers were encouraged to join in the verbal attacks, taunting the members of my family. While she was being subjected to

Maturing reforested meadow near the reservoir

such torment, my mother was forced to keep her head covered and to look down at the ground. I remember her telling me that she was glad that now that I had returned, she could lift her eyes and look directly in my face.

Those were such strange and difficult times. I remember well my half-brother explaining to local officials on my first visit that I had left Golok well before the Chinese takeover, so I should not be treated as someone who had escaped Chinese rule. Yet it took a long time for my mother to talk about these

South apple orchard near Cintamani Temple

things. "Do not ask me any questions about those times," she would say to me. Like many who endure great suffering, she simply did not want to have to recall what had happened.

My visits back to Tibet only increased my commitment to making Odiyan a Dharma Realm of unsurpassed beauty. I had come so far, and seen so many things I had never imagined to exist when I was a boy. Now I felt it was my duty to make my journey worthwhile: for the sake of my parents and my beloved teachers, and for the sake of the tradition and the people of Tibet, who cherished the Dharma over so many centuries.

Magnolia about to open in the Chapel garden

The Nyingma tradition has always stood out in Tibet for the prominent role play by lay practitioners who married and lived the life of a householder. There were some who criticized the Nyingma school on these grounds, saying that such masters could not be perfect teachers or form a true Sangha. My own view, however, is that the Nyingma lay masters stand in the lineage of King Indrabodhi and the great Siddhas, accomplished masters who showed how enlightenment was possible in all circumstances. Guru Padmasambhava continued that tradition, and it is worth noting that many of his best disciples were women, including the incomparable Yeshe Tsogyal, who

White peony in full bloom at the Chapel

wrote down and preserved his teachings for later generations of Terma Masters to recover. I still have in my possession a text written in her own hand that preserves the advice that Trisong Detsen gave to practitioners, and I cherish it as a great treasure.

These are the roots of the heritage that I carry within me, passed on by my parents, my teachers, and my culture. For decades now, I have been working to transplant those roots to a new land. I have always looked in two directions at once:

Apples in the south orchard

preserving the traditions and wisdom of Tibet and supporting the Sangha, while at the same time communicating what I could of the Dharma in a new land. Somehow I was picked up like an arrow notched to a bow and shot 7,000 miles to the west, landing in unknown corners with an unknown destiny before me. I cannot ignore that call. It is my duty, my responsibility, my mission to make sure that what I received is not lost. I hope that those who have been loyal to me for so long, and those who come after, will work toward that same goal.

are ready for harvesting

Time moves quickly, and we all need to ask what we can do in the time we have left. In one way, the answer is clear. Be an example. Be a master. Be a teacher. Manage the resources available to you. Care for Odiyan, share your knowledge, write books. I have had no time to teach publicly for almost forty years now, but you, my students can teach. Here you have a great advantage over me. You know the language; you know the ways of thinking. There is much you can do.

There are times when I feel that I have been acting out a special destiny. At other times, I take a more humble view,

Grazing time for mother and baby Joy

for it is clear to me that I am simply acting on the duty I owe my parents, my teachers, my students, and my friends. Either way, I have no choice but to do as I have done. Having started on this path, I have been consistent in the choices I have made. I have done my best to stay loyal to my own work and the efforts of those who trust me.

I have little insight and limited experience, and my ability to speak Western language and interact with Western culture and ways of knowing are limited as well. Still, I try. I do not know much, but I pretend—and my pretending has had results.

An affectionate moment with newborn mini and mother

A Vision of Reality

When we first set out to create the Copper Mountain Mandala of Odiyan, my students knew very little of Oddiyana or the symbols of the mandala. Had we been able to look forward from 1975 to the present day, the beauty of Odiyan would have seems an impossible dream. Yet the dream is now real. That is the power of the mind: it has no shape or form, but it can create meaningful shapes and forms. It can offer the heart and senses a new way of being.

Almost forty years ago, when I published *Time, Space, and Knowledge*, I called it "a new vision of reality." Here at Odiyan, we live in such a new vision of reality. It is one thing to live in virtual reality, something I am told may soon be possible, but it is another thing entirely to live in a vision of reality that expresses virtue. Our ancestors created such a virtuous reality, and so did the great artists and religious masters down through the centuries. Everyone has dreams and fantasies, but if dreams are based on knowledge, and if people are willing to work to make them real, inspiring new visions can take form. With the help of friends and supporters, that is what has happened at Odiyan. Conducted by invisible knowledge, a new reality has come into being.

I arrived in this country with little knowledge of what to expect and almost no resources. The West knew very little of Buddhism, and I lacked any understanding of how this new culture operated. Yet my students and I set to work, and through our consistent efforts and commitment, the shape and form of the mandala became visible.

Peony blossoms in the Stupa courtyard

In a way, this is the story of countless immigrants to America, the Land of Opportunity. I myself came from a land located almost at the opposite end of the earth. I brought with me my lineage, the blessings of my family and teachers, and the training I had received from great masters. My love for the Dharma and the heritage of Tibet allowed my heart to accommodate a new vision, and my mind helped to give that vision form. Now I dare to hope that what we have created here will last for a long time to come.

Main Temple viewed from the Cherry Mall

This country, for all its difficulties, has an inner stability, and its impact on the rest of the world is far-reaching. The reach of American culture continues to expand. The American ideals of freedom of religion and speech and its commitment to equality of opportunity are honored globally. For me, having arrived here as a hopeless refugee, these are not just abstract principles. The vision of this country's founders is a vital part of the reality I have lived and the vision I have sought to create. Because this promise still lives in America,

Path to the aviary in Mandala Garden

Odiyan and the Buddhist heritage have the opportunity to embody a rich future.

Odiyan is a gesture of gratitude to this land and its people, and a symbol of what is possible. It is also a gesture of appreciation for my friends and students, and for this beautiful land, a place to cherish always. Even our neighbors appreciate the work we have done to protect and restore the land, the hundreds of thousands of trees we have planted, the conservation efforts we have mounted, and our dedication to preserving Odiyan's

Walnut tree ready for autumn harvesting

natural beauty. Odiyan's riches give me great joy, and I am happy to share that joy with others.

I have always also thought of Odiyan and the monuments and sacred forms we have created, displayed, and buried here as a form of protection from natural disasters. I pray each day that the prayer flags, prayer wheels, tsa tsas, and empowerments; the mantras, Sutras, and prayers, will counter the demonic forces that seem to have been unleashed on the world, the anger, hatred, and crazy emotionality that we have all

Mini horses enjoy the Redwood grove, near the Stupa

witnessed through the media or in person. It is difficult to know for certain whether such efforts have an impact, but at least we can say that the intention is positive.

In the last few decades, the Nagas and the Lokapalas have shown in countless ways, through earthquakes, floods, hurricanes, and more, that they are not happy, and the sheer power of the weapons we have developed truly concerns me. Perhaps our efforts can counteract such negative and destructive forces. That is the teaching of my heritage, and I truly hope it is so. I honor and express these wishes not only

A variety of apples grow in the many orchards

here at Odiyan, but in our work restoring the sacred places of the Dharma, erecting peace bells at holy sites, and sponsoring hundreds of ceremonies, including the annual World Peace Ceremony at Bodh Gaya, where 15,000 people or more gather to generate positive energy.

Having arrived here with so little, I cannot believe myself the scope of what we have been able to accomplish. Some who landed on these shores as refugees could think only of survival and security, but for me, the dream of preserving my own culture and the blessings of the Dharma were fundamental.

Pomegranates nearing harvest in the east orchard

That is why it gives me such joy to know that all our organizations have made real contributions. I never tire of pointing out the millions of books we have printed and distributed, the 130 titles we have published in English, many translated into other languages, the teachings I have developed for these times, such as Kum Nye, Skillful Means, and the Time, Space, and Knowledge Vision. All these are tangible accomplishments. They benefit people today, and they can continue to do so in the future.

Pink azeleas in Mandala Garden

Odiyan adds to these accomplishments. It is a home for the Dharma and for our small community. It is also a symbol of all we have done and of what might happen in the future. The Odiyan mandala contains within it manifestations of the Eight Great Bodhisattvas and the five Dhyani Buddhas. I hope that all who live at Odiyan can invite them into their hearts as well, for without such blessings, we may not survive.

This book is a way of expressing my hopes and dreams and reflecting on how they have manifested in time. We have built

Brilliant mound of chrysanthemums at the Chapel

Odiyan in the west of the West, but it is an offering for all humanity, a Sukhavati field of happiness and virtue, and a garden of delights. Odiyan shows that even a refugee like me can accomplish something of real value. I hope that my family, friends, and students, reflecting on what we been able to do here, will always acknowledge the greatness of a country that makes such achievements possible.

As for myself, I can take satisfaction in what we have done. I came here with a dream and a vision, and I did not fail.

Fragrant red rose in the Stupa garden

Joined by my students, family, and friends, I have left behind a footprint in the sands of time. As a community, we have dedicated our time and energy—even our whole lives—to creating Odiyan and all that it represents. Some might call this faith. Whatever happens now, we can say that we stand for something, and that we have been prepared to act on our beliefs. As Americans say, we walk our talk. Having created something of value, we know in our heart of hearts that our lives have not been wasted.

A peppermint rose in Vairocana Garden

Final Reflections

When we look honestly, we see the signs of suffering everywhere—in the lives of others and in our own lives as well. It is natural to ask what we can do in the face of all this sorrow, this frustration and unhappiness. We recognize the workings of karma and experience the results for ourselves. How shall we respond? How can we reverse this powerful momentum?

In a sense, the question answers itself. What we are lacking is the knowledge we need to respond effectively. It is this knowledge we must discover and activate. Who can doubt that if we knew how the causes and conditions that shape our lives manifest, we could take action? Perhaps we could make a real difference, for ourselves and also for others.

The place to begin is by looking at the patterns through which our lives unfold—the workings of karma and klesha. Let us trace out one way of doing so, of analyzing what goes on in experience.

A crisp breeze brings signs of spring to the east entryway.

How our World Arises

It seems we are caught in the grip of forces we cannot control, like a mouse picked up and dropped into a cage. First we experience, then we identify what we experience, and then we respond to what we have identified. It is a pattern that leaves no opportunity for freedom and little opportunity for joy.

In Buddhism, this basic pattern is sometimes described in terms of the operation of the five skandhas: rupa, vedana,

Path towards Mandala Garden

samjna, samskara, and vijnana. First a situation presents itself (rupa). Before we really know what is happening, we respond in terms of liking, disliking, or indifference (vedana). With our mind already predisposed to react in a certain way, we identify, perceive, and recognize (samjna). Now our karmic conditioning kicks in, and the full power of our habitual patterns takes hold (samskara). On this basis, the situation is known; it is set in place (vijnana). The case has been made and judgment has been rendered: the truth of the matter is established. The die is cast. Nothing can be done.

Old bay trees and hydrangeas in North Park

This established reality has certain inevitable structures. It is a fundamentally dualistic system, in which the 'subject-I' reacts to the 'object-contents'. The initial reaction happens beyond our ability to control it: we like and dislike, move toward or push away. From these basic feelings, the links proceed through impressions to perceptions and identifications. The identifications find expression in words and labels, creating the basis for action and reaction and the specification of reality.

Evergreen trees planted over the last 40 years

All this is automatic. I cannot dismiss what I perceive to be so, and I cannot question the labels that assign identity. What is formed and cast is recognized, identified, and given to consciousness. No other interpretation is possible. Just as a magnetic force pulls metal toward a magnet, so the momentum of samsaric patterning shapes reality through the power of our interpretations. We could say that the world that comes into being has its own 'magnetude'.

Through this magnetude, I am assigned the role of the subject. I am the one who pronounces the truth of what I have identified, applies the label, confirms the manifestation, and responds with whatever judgments are suitable and fitting. The attachment or aversion I experience, along with positive or negative emotions, arises as part of this process. Whatever does not conform to these responses, I reject or simply ignore. If that response is not available, I may feel confused or uncertain. When this happens, something may quickly shift—in the next moment I am distracted, pulled away in some other direction. The result may be that the initial moment never fully takes form,

In the Aviary: peahen with her chicks

leaving me unable to say what has really happened. I may not even notice that anything has happened at all.

When identity does move to completion, I respond accordingly. I am angry or upset, or I react with words or gestures. Either way, what has been defined in this way shapes my world. I may recognize an enemy that prevents me from getting what I want. I may get angry or agitated. Reacting based on fundamental patterns, I interpret what happens—actions, manifestations, gestures—in predictable ways.

Guardians of Cintamani Lake

When such patterns lead to suffering, there is nothing I can do about it. I cannot refuse to go along, because my perceptions, my language, and the quality and character of my reactions all fit with what I am experiencing. I am caught in the magnetude of what appears. The language icon and the sense impressions that pop up all lead to the same place. Just as fire burns, so attachment, anger, and every form of emotionality play themselves out. Our actions carry on, even if they leave us feeling miserable. We cannot call a halt.

Horses graze in the spacious meadows

In this pervasive dynamic, language plays a central role. The labels I assign linguistically empower appearance through the mechanisms of identity and definition. Language introduces meanings, shaping the world and confirming the subject who assigns the meanings. The subject determines, and the mind responds, saying "Yes!" No separation between subject and object is possible—I am bonded to what appears. From one perspective, the object is presented to the subject, which receives and acknowledges what is presented. From another perspec-

beyond the perimeter fence

tive, the subject (as one pole in the magnetude)—projects onto the object (as the other pole) whatever ideas and concepts it has available. Drawn together, subject and object interact, and the interaction has its own distinctive feel; for instance, anger, desire, or some specific form of emotionality.

All this forms the situation I find myself in. Bonded to subject-object relations, I have no other place to go. A background identity generates meanings and definitions for subject and object alike. An instant seeing captures the particulars of what manifests, and a response arises. The response is identified in

Narcissus flowers along Stupa road

turn, and core identity takes form. The identity supports the dynamic of grasping along with residues that will help shape what comes next, and the whole is established.

As for the 'I' it is completely engaged in this whole, involved as the subject in whatever object or objective situation manifests. A situation is operating, inside me and outside as well, and I cannot separate one meaning from any other. If I am attached or upset or confused or depressed; if I experience suffering of any kind, I have no way to escape.

Roses in bloom at the Main Temple

We might imagine that if our analysis helped us identify these patterns—if we could see how labels and identities lead to character, shape, and form, such understanding could create an opening to break free of samsaric patterns. In that sense, the kind of analysis we are doing here may be helpful. Yet at a deeper level, where greater understanding might make a real difference, knowledge remains lacking. We do not have a deeper understanding of the meaning of 'subject' and 'object'. We don't understand the label 'mind' or the meaning of mind. We

Evergreens surround the cherry mall

cannot explore in new ways the object of appearance or the meaning of appearance, or investigate the deeper significance of 'shape' and 'form' and 'content'. We cannot trace the beginning, middle, and end of how appearance arises. We don't even know how to ask such questions. What happens simply happens—we don't know how it happens, and at some level we don't even know what happened, because happening happens almost instantly. The only 'coming from' operates at the level of explanation, arising after the fact.

as cherry trees burst into bloom

With no other way to know, there is little to say about our suffering and the operations of karma. We may speak of habits or the nature of mind as conditioned to operate in certain ways. We may explain that the senses and the act of perception have their own unique character and position. Yet really we are saying there is nothing to be done.

Once we operate with this understanding, there is no antidote for samsara, which is just the way things are. We cannot con-

Spring in the Chapel garden includes

trol our situation or our reactions. We cannot separate mind from its operations, cannot separate the subjective feeling of attraction from the object to which we are attracted. We like to imagine that we are living our lives moment by moment in the present, but it may be more accurate to say that we are living in the past, in a world that has already been established. We might like to choose a better way to live, but the choice has already been made. It is too late. Suffering is built in, just as heat is built into fire.

a wide variety of plants, trees and shrubs

If we are confused about this, if we cherish the hope that we could free ourselves from suffering, it may be because we are used to thinking of ourselves as separate individuals, as subjects independent of the objects we encounter in the world. Yet the relations between subject and object—their magnetude—is powerful. It binds us completely, like the force of gravity that keeps us bound to the earth.

This suggests that our sense of separation and independence may be mistaken. Once the skandhas are in operation, each conditions the others, and there is no separating them. The subject relies on certain faculties, and each faculty has its own

Leyland Cyprus near the Chapel

rhythms that ripple through the whole of experience. Each new moment gives its own 'from' and 'to', its own beginnings and endings—at least, that is what our beliefs tell us.

We seem to operate in a field that extends around us in all directions, both mental and physical. Within that field, the power of magnetude binds together every element. As soon as we identify, we have guaranteed and presupposed the pronouncement of what is so. The perception is formed, and the judgments of pro and con, right and wrong, like and dislike are performed. Is there something deeper than that? In this way of understanding, this pattern of operation, we cannot say.

Prayer flags and evergreens line the road near Mandala Garden.

A Different Journey

Let us imagine a different possibility. Suppose that within the structured field of experience there is an operator—like an engine that powers the field's unfolding. That operator might manifest a certain knowing quality, a seeing that radiates light: transparent, invisible, but active. Just as the formless openness or emptiness of space allows form and beauty to appear, such a light would allow perceptions, sense experience, concepts, and the identities of appearance to manifest.

These manifestations are the reality we inhabit—the relative truth we know to be so. But now we are allowing for another way of seeing. What if we could look directly at the operator. Since the operator powers the field, we can imagine that we would not find a 'from' or 'to'. In the realm where the operator operates, the structures we accept as real would not have taken form.

We do not have to accept this image of the operator, or even try to go to that level of 'perception' through meditation or awareness. Just the idea that we could reach a level where our relative truth does not operate has its own power. Once we allow for that possibility, we can approach our present reality in a different way.

Think of your life as a journey. We can call it that because it has a beginning and an end: we come into the world and we will pass out of it. In the usual way of seeing, our journey will proceed from one fixed point to another. Yet if our relative truth is not the only truth, if reality is not fixed, we are free

to consider a different kind of journey. How can we plan the best possible journey? How can we set out on a path where we do not encounter obstacles or distractions, what the Buddhist tradition calls Marayas. How can we enter a world not shaped by karma and klesha?

If we knew how to conduct our journey in a positive way, a way that causes no harm, would karma be able to interfere? Is

Looking toward Cintamani from the reservoir

there a vision that can guide us? This is the possibility we have already considered. If we understand something about the way things have been in the past and how they have come to be, we may know how to operate in the present. We may know how to move toward the goal that we have set for our journey. We may be able to lay out a path where the road is pleasant and open rather than rocky, a path free from frustration, agitation, distraction, and obstacles.

Field of incense cedars and redwoods

At present, our journey and the journey that all beings undertake, is full of difficulty and tragedies at every level. We suffer in our minds and bodies, we suffer in our relations with friends and family, we see for ourselves the conflicts between neighbors, citizens and countries. If we want to set out on a different journey, free from karmic conditioning—a journey that is useful, positive, challenging, and transforming—we will have to put in place a skillful method. Even more fundamentally,

Looking west from Vajra Temple

we will need to develop more knowledge, leading to new vision. Looking at the past, we will need to know how knowing itself arises and takes form. Looking at the present, we will need to be clear about the relationship between subject and object. We will need to know the 'who' of who I am, and know what it means to live in an 'I-ness' society, a 'self-ness' society, an observation society, an instructor society.

Reforested trees merge with the native forest

To navigate the pathways that will shape our journey, we will need to be our own tour guide. Our perceptions will need to be trustworthy, and we will need to know how to take the long view. We will need to see accurately, to know the weather, the terrain, and the social customs of the land we are passing through, and we will need to be ready to take on challenges as they arise.

Are we able to serve as tour guide for our own journey? Are we knowledgeable in the right ways? Can we be the trustworthy one, leading our awareness, our consciousness, our expe-

Mimosa blossoms

rience, and our perceptions in positive directions? These are fundamental questions, for if we cannot be flexible, or if we lack the right motivation, our journey may stay strictly within the realm of what is already established and accepted.

In the journey that is already underway, we find ourselves traveling through the domains of fear and worry and paranoia. We confront the unexpected, and we lack the knowledge to challenge what appears. But we can shape our journey in accord with a deeper, richer knowledge. We can make it into a path of valuable transitions, leading gently toward transformation.

East Orchard Iris

When the journey unfolds as a path of transformation, it will be more open, more flexible. We will find ourselves able to stay in full contact with every situation we encounter. Our experiences may seem more like beautiful dreams, or like inherently interesting images. We will turn them readily toward the artistic, the creative, and the transformative, and we will manifest the love of beauty. We will travel a path rich in positivity and free from all bondage.

North Chapel gardens display

For a long time, for time before we can recall, we have been wandering on a rocky and bleak terrain, gathering and fiercely grasping at the few jewels we encounter along the way, half-obscured by dust and dirt. But we are free to enter the depths of a different way of knowing, where experience itself is more fulfilling and life more valuable. On this path of freedom, subject and object alike manifest creatively. No longer eking out a living, like the owner of a business selling what no one wants in

a diversity of thriving plantlife

a place where people seldom come, we can simply draw on the riches that are always available, effortlessly enjoying a wealth that never diminishes.

To live in this way is easy and deeply nourishing. Yet making the transition requires a very different understanding from the one that guides our usual samsaric activity. My suggestion is that you do your best to make this transition. Train yourself

Indisputable determination of wildflowers at Odiyan

day and night in how to take the easy way, even if at first it looks difficult. You can make your journey and the events it presents into the source of fulfillment. You may not avoid suffering, but if you understand the nature of the mind, you will have access to the knowledge you need, ready to respond flexibly and in the direction of joy. Whether your experience is negative or positive will not matter. Even feeling dull or distracted will be an opportunity to make the journey richer.

Pansies grow through the tiles at the Main Temple

How you operate the journey of your life depends on the attitudes you develop and on how you prepare yourself for whatever comes next. Set yourself a goal that is worthy of your potential, whether you call it a vision, a view, a plan, or even a dream. Commit yourself to self-understanding, and you will discover a path free from resistance, a way that is at once profound and profoundly easy.

Spring peonies in bloom

Nobody is binding or restricting you. You are free from the control of each and every regime. The operation is in your hands, and it is up to you to create the kind of journey you want.

Iceplant along Stupa road

Self-Mastery

The path we follow on this journey is a path of self-mastery. It does not depend on reading books or on thinking about every instant of experience. Our life unfolds what it has to offer us on its own terms. We simply see what is there, and see as well that we are making the meaning of 'thereness', of 'identityness', of 'selfness'. These are all points that we ourselves are making. At first we do so in an immediate way, but eventually we do so symbolically as well.

Once we understand how points are related to meanings, we can open different points and different meanings: different points of view, different ways of looking, and different interpretations. We are no longer stuck in dark corners or frightening alleyways; we are no longer prisoners. We can free what is frozen—free the structures that come with the structure of subject and object. We have grown used to always looking down at the ground, stumbling along, but when we learn to lift our heads, we may realize that we have known all along how to fly. This 'uplifting' is what is sometimes called liberation. It comes when we have the right attitude, take the right angle, and follow the right way.

It is legitimate to reply: "Tell me more. What is this way, this attitude? How do I develop it?" But asking these questions may not be the right approach. Once we start to practice a different way of operating the journey, logic and language are no longer the best guide. They do not fit the need. Instead, the question to ask is more immediate: Is the job getting done? Right now, am I caught in the old patterns?

Pyracantha berry shrub at the Chapel

Searching for the right answer or the right direction, can leave us going round in circles and loops forever, confronting the same problems. This is the way we know already. It goes along with the ways we already have for viewing, receiving, presenting, questioning, and thinking. It may not get us where we hope to go.

Now we are looking for a different way, an independent way, one that does not follow the same patterns. Right now, we have the ability to offer ourselves liberation, and we deserve the opportunity to accept this gift.

Clear faced pansies and johnny jump ups

What is the difference, in the end? If we read books on philosophy or follow the ways handed down to us by a tradition or follow the course of action the mind presents, we limit ourselves to one reality. Yet there are many realities, many possible ways. This is not some esoteric knowledge: it is the simple truth of our situation. Human beings have been on this earth for millions of years, and it makes little sense to say that all of them have followed the same understanding or inhabited the same reality. Even today, whenever just a few people gather, they will have different ways to understand, different ways to cure, to manifest, and to embody the meaning of our journey through life.

Pink peonies of spring

The difference, then, is clear. If the journey we undertake proves rich, healthy, and positive, our passage through life will be worthwhile. If not, if we find ourselves following the pathways of anger, destruction, disappointment, and disillusionment, what is the point?

Seeing that this is so, we need to prepare well. Because we have been taught a dualistic way of being, we are caught in our present situation. We follow the given ways: the mind way,

senses way, thoughts way, concept way, 'I-ness' way, and 'I' way. Now we can ask, face to face: what is the meaning of the points that we take for granted?

As soon as we look directly, we find openness. There are possibilities and dimensions other than what we believe, and a new-light knowledge is available, a new partnership, a new way to embody ourselves in our actions. This is a unique opportunity, and we cannot afford to let it go by.

Trees planted over thirty years ago grow tall.

We already hold precious jewels in our hands. Perhaps now we can see that this is so. We can recognize that we have better weapons, better antidotes, better ways of transformation—beyond what ordinary leaders and teachers and doctors have to offer us. We can retransform our situation. If we connect with that possibility, a new frontier is available, a new world and a new universe. We can make our senses, our thoughts, and our minds into new friends, letting them find new ways to communicate and transform. That is the new journey we can undertake—the journey of self-mastery.

Bright yellow Persian buttercup

My hope and my wish is that you set out on this journey, and that you make for yourself a path that does not force you through confusion and disillusionment. You can be self-sufficient, starting where you are right now. You do not need to carry out analytical examinations of what is so. You do not need to request the 'hows' of your own experience. It is enough to take ease and to let yourself know.

Fragrant freesias in the rim maple bed

As you put this way of being into effect, you may suspect that your efforts are incomplete, even artificial. That is fine. Once in a while, as the journey unfolds, you may have the sense that things are perfect as they are, and that is enough to start. It is certainly better than negativity, grumpiness, dark, dull resentment, loneliness, and anger. All such manifestations have nothing to offer you. Let go of them; let them float away like clouds. Simply imitating what you sense is possible is a good beginning.

Birches and viburnum in the outer lawn

Right now, and from time to time as you go forward, you can offer yourself positive feelings and an open freedom. Taste this; test it; exercise it. Even if you are just pretending, go ahead. As you do, you are making body impressions and language gestures, and you will be opening new sensory fields. You are letting go of the patterns you have been holding on to.

Cherry Mall in bloom

We all manifest strong behaviors and patterns that shape our character. Like gravity, they hold us down. Now is the time to ask whether we could switch. Can we exercise our being in a new way, light and loose? Can we just forget about all the negativity? Can we ask ourselves in a fresh, new way why we experience so much unhappiness? Why not give ourselves and others hope and positive loving feelings? Why not aim to accommodate ourselves, at ease and at home?

Main Temple mound garden

In this culture, people often look for companions to share their lives, and hope in this way to open their hearts. Yet your companion may not always be there for you. It seems better to provide for yourself the support you need. You can offer yourself cheer and good thoughts. These are some of the precious jewels that you already possess. When you manifest them, others will be drawn toward you, and you will have a positive impact on them as well. After all, it is always pleasant to be with someone whose outlook is positive.

Main temple gardens in spring

We are used to thinking of our own concerns and needs, but this self that we cherish is a self that is enslaved to patterns that run its life. If we give up on that rigid self, we can be more flexible and free. That is not just nice words: it really is true. At any time we can change our impressions, our gestures, our tone of voice, our language, and the ways we relate. These may seem like small, simple steps, but they have real consequences. Your energy becomes more inviting, and you have the pleasure of knowing that you are doing a good job.

Red peony blooming among the yellow daisies

None of this has to do with deep spiritual realizations but it does make a difference. Here in this community, there are many ways to see how this works. Your attitude, how you work together, how you are at meals—these are memorable influences, more fulfilling for both you and others. Americans have an expression: "What have you got in your pocket?" Our pockets are not full, but we can offer instead a good heart and good thoughts. We can be helpful to each other. We can create a place to play, a place of meaning, in this community and as a model for future generations. That is something that this country and these times badly need.

Vibrant colored lilies of summer

Merit and Dedication

The Abhidharma teachings of Buddhism speak in terms of body, mind, and spirit, consciousness, awareness, and actions. The classification into the five skandhas comes out of these teachings. These forms of analysis are important, but in our community we also follow higher teachings. In our way of practicing Dharma, our work and our way of life form a mandala of Dharma activity. They manifest our positive thoughts and the virtue of the path. It is a path of beauty, for it is always meritorious.

The concept of merit is not known in Western traditions, and it may be some time before it is understood at a deeper level. Yet Western traditions do know about good deeds, sincere conduct, virtue, and living a valuable life. They know about good thoughts, kindness, and positive intentions. All this seems to be universal. It describes well the path we have set out to follow.

Even without going into the teachings on merit, it is easy to see that some people are happier and healthier than others. Somehow there are causal circumstances at work that lead to benefit and well-being. We guide our lives in accord with this principle, understood in accord with the teachings of the Buddha. We work to transform selfish and limited ways of being into conduct carried out for the sake of others. We are not perfect Bodhisattvas, but we do have good intentions and the wish to dedicate our efforts to the welfare of others and the preservation of priceless knowledge.

Tree roses at Cintamani gardens rise up to the golden stupas

Most people who have worked in our community know little about Buddhist symbols or Buddhist philosophy. Yet there are elements in Buddhism that resonate with all religious traditions: prayers, initiations, sacred temples and sanctuaries, recitation, and meditation. Some of these ideas and symbols are familiar to almost everyone. Even more important, everyone understands that there can be conduct that unites us in the spirit of goodness. Every religion teaches this, and even those who follow no religion may be open to similar ideas.

Double Delight Rose in the Temple garden

The Buddhist tradition has always admired those who act with good intentions, whether they follow a particular religious path or not. That is how we practice. The benefit for ourselves is that we eventually learn to let go of guilt, toxic emotionality, and karmic garbage. In a way, we sacrifice our own well-being, but in another way, we benefit tremendously. Through our work and our devotion to what we are doing, we are paying off karmic debts. Even if we make mistakes, even if our intentions are not always completely positive, I truly believe that the Buddhas, the Bodhisattvas, and Guru Padmasambhava look upon us and bless our conduct.

Roses glow on trees and bushes at the Stupa

We do not have to accept this on faith. We can see for ourselves the tangible, meritorious results of our actions. We have preserved the treasures of an ancient culture and restored them to those who can benefit most. We have put down roots here in the West that we hope will continue to grow and bear fruit for a long time to come. In today's world, the benefits of mindfulness, cultivating inner calm and compassion, and similar forms of Buddhist practice are widely acknowledged, but I would say that our way of practice offers benefits at least as great. We are learning how to live a meaningful life, and how to use inquiry as a path toward transformation. Whether you continue

Rhododendron trees flowering in Mandala Garden

to work with us or not, these lessons will stay with you, and you will know that you did your part.

There is a saying in Tibet that a single tear drop that falls in the ocean will never disappear as long as the oceans exist. In the same way, a single meritorious act will continue to spread its benefits through all of time. We have made this our path, contributing our energy, our intelligence, and our resources for a good cause, not only for the people of Tibet, but for sentient beings everywhere.

Orchids thrive outside the offices in the north rim

We live in dangerous times, and all the world needs blessings. Our work serves that purpose. It benefits beings everywhere, whether they are alive today or have already passed on. We have worked on their behalf, and we will continue to do so for as long as we can. The Dharma is in its infancy in the West, but we have created a kind of model for how it could contribute to this culture. It is a model that relies on selfless, total

Japanese maples offer hues of orange and red in autumn

dedication, on a transforming vision, and on working for a good cause. It seems to me a good model, but whether others take it up or not, I believe that what we have done will last a long time, benefiting others and also benefiting each of you. Ours is a community where we are mostly happy, healthy, and fulfilled. Surely the blessings of our work are a part of the reason why this is so.

The calmness of the pond mirrors the temples and landscape.

I wish to express my deep appreciation to all of you in the community and to acknowledge the role that America, with its undying commitment to freedom of religion, has played in making our work possible. I dedicate the merits of the Odiyan Copper Mountain Mandala to all who have volunteered here or supported our efforts in other ways, and to the future generations who enter this mandala.

If we had tried to do what we have done while paying normal wages, we could not have accomplished even a small part of what we have been able to achieve. Because you have worked faithfully and with devotion, we have done great things, and I fully believe that Guru Padmasambhava and the Great Bodhisattvas rain down their blessings on all of you, and that your meritorious actions will follow you.

May each of you receive the blessings of the lineage, and may your family, relatives, and friends share in your positive karma. May they and you experience a beautiful life, now and forever, living in peace and joy, completely free from karmic obscurations, and securely embarked on the path of transformation. Just as the prayer wheels, prayer flags, and sacred forms of the Odiyan mandala release billions of prayers each day into the cosmos, so may the power of your positive actions radiate out into your lives and into the lives of all beings, now and forever.

White Irises brighten the Cherry Mall in spring

Odiyan Gardens

Trees and Plants

1	Abelia grandiflora 'Edward Goucher'	R
2	Abies concolor grandis	MG
3	Abies koreana	C
4	Abutilon hybridium	C
5	Acacia baileyana 'purpurea'	MG,L,S
6	Acacia melanoxyloss	L
7	Acacia fornesiana	L
8	Acer buergerarnum	N,PR
9	Acer capillipes	VG
10	Acer ginnala	NP,R
11	Acer japonicum 'aconitifolium', 'Maiku Jaku', 'Junihitoye', 'Kinkakure', 'O Isame'	R
12	Acer macropyhyllum	NP,R
13	Acer palmatum 'shigitatsu sawa', 'Atropurpurea', 'Atropurpurea dissectum,' 'Ayoyagi', 'Bene Schichihenge', 'Bene Otake', 'Bloodgood', 'Butterfly', 'Crimson Queen', 'Ever Red', 'Filigree', 'Garnet', 'Higasayama', 'Kasagiyama', 'Kiyohime', 'Okushimo', 'Omurayama', 'Orido Nishiki', 'Red Select', 'Sagara Nishiki', 'Sango Kaku', 'Seiryu', 'Seikimori', 'Shindeshojo', 'Shishigashira', 'Tana', 'Trompenburg', 'Viridis dissectum', 'Waterfall', seedlings of palmatums	R R,C,MG
14	Acer pentaphyllum	R

15	Acer shirasawanum 'Palmatifolium'	R
16	Acer pseudopiatanus 'Spaethii'	R
17	Acer rubrum	R
18	Aesculus californicum	NP
19	Aesculus x carnea	
20	Ajuga reptans	
21	Albizia julibrissin	C,VT
22	Almond 'Ne Plus Ultra', 'Non Pariel'	L
23	Alnus coratra	MG
24	Alyogyne huegelii	NP
25	Anemone x hybrida	S
26	Anigozanthos flavidus	R
27	Apple 'Arkansas Black orchard', 'Ashmead's Kernel', 'Black Twig', 'Bramley's Seedling', 'Calville Blanc de Hive', 'Cox Orange Pippin', 'Fuji', 'Gala', 'Golden Delicious', 'Granny Smith', 'Graven', 'Idared', 'Jonagold', 'Liberty', 'Macoun', 'McIntosh', 'Mutsu', 'Newton Pippin', 'Northern Spy', 'Pink Pearl', 'Red Delicious', 'Rome Beauty', 'Sierra Beauty', 'Spitzenberg', 'Stayman Winesap', 'Wagener', 'Winter Banana', 'Yellow Bellflower'	L
28	Apricot 'Autumn Royal', 'Sweet Kernel', 'Moorpark', 'Royal Blenheim'	L
29	Araia elata	MG
30	Aralia sieboldii	
31	Araucaria araucana	
32	Arbutus 'Marina'	S,MG
33	Arbutus menziestii	L,MG
34	Arbutus unedo 'Compacta'	C,L,R

35	Arcotostaphylos manzanita	MG
36	Astilbe x ardensii	C
37	Aucuba 'Crotonifolia', 'Fructo Alba'	MG
38	Aucuba japonica	
39	Bambusa darwinii	NP
40	Berberis thunbergii 'Atropurpurea', 'Rose Glow'	MG
41	Bergenia hybrids	S
42	Betula maximowicziana	R
43	Betula pendula	NP
44	Bougainvillea	C
45	Buddleia davidii	MG,S
46	Buxus microphylla japonica 'Green Beauty'	R,C,CT,S,VT,L
47	Buxus sempervierens 'Arborescens', 'Aureo-varietaga'	S
48	Cactaceae and aloes	L
49	Calluna vulgaris, 'Robert Chapman', 'Silver Queen'	C,L
50	Calocedrus decurrens	VT,S,P,L
51	Camellia japonica cultivars	S,C ,L,P
52	Camillia sasanqua 'Cleopatra'	R
53	Carex	R
54	Carpinus betulus	R,CT
55	Castanea mollissima x dentata	L
	Ceanothus 'Anchor Bay', 'Blue Jeans', 'Concha', 'Dark Star', 'Frosty Blue', 'Julia Phelps', 'Louis Edmonds',	

56	'Ray Hartman', 'Snow Flurry', 'Snowball', 'Yankee Point'	MG,C,L
57	Cedrus atlantica 'Galuca'	R
58	Cedrus deodara, 'Cream Puff', 'Descanso Dwarf'	CT,S
59	Cercidiphyllum japonicum	VG,MG,R
60	Cercis candensis, 'Forest Pansy'	R
61	Cercis occidentalis	MG
62	Cercis reniformis 'Oklahoma'	MG
63	Chaenomeles species 'Jet Trail', 'Tall Red', 'Toyo Nishiki'	R,NP
64	Chamaecyparis lawsoniana 'Elwoodii Improved'	NP,R
65	Chamaecyparis 'Nidiformis'	R
66	Chamaecyparis obtusa 'Gracilis', 'Graciosa', 'Kosteri', 'Nana Lutea', 'Sanderi', 'Wells Special'	NP
67	Chamaecyparis pisifera 'Boulevard', 'Filifera Nana Aurea', 'Snow', 'Squarrosa Intermedia', 'Squarrosa Veichii'	
68	Cherry 'Bing', 'Lambert', 'Montmorency', 'Ranier', 'Royal Ann', 'Sam', 'Stella', 'Van'	L
69	Chionanthus retusus	NP
70	Chitalpa tashkentensis	VT
71	Choisya ternata	MG,R
72	Cistus hybridus	NP,L
73	Cistus salvifolius	S,NP
74	Cistus skanbergii	NP
75	Citrus 'Owari Satsuma'	C,R
76	Coleonema album	VT

77	Coleonema pulchrum 'Sunset Gold'	S,CT
78	Cornus capitata	NP,R
79	Cornus controversa	R
80	Cornus 'Edie's White Wonder'	NP
81	Cornus florida	NP
82	Cornus kousa 'Koreana'	MG
83	Cornus nuttallii	
84	Corokia cotoneaster	VT
85	Corylus colurna	R
86	Corylus maxima	PR
87	Cotinus coggygria 'Purpureus'	VT
88	Cotoneaster horizontalis	VT
89	Cotoneaster perpusilla 'Variegatus'	VT
90	Cotoneaster salicifolia	VT
91	Crataegus phaenophrum	S,R
92	Cryptomeria japonica 'Elegans compacta', 'Lobbi Nana', 'Nana', seedlings	C,NP,CT
93	Cupressocyparis leylandii 'Castlewellan'	VT
94	Cupressus glabra	PR
95	Cupressus macrocarpa	CT
96	Cupressus sempervirens	S
97	Cytisus kewensis	NP
98	Cytisus lydia	S
99	Daboecia cantrcrica 'Alba'	C,S
100	Daphne odora 'Marginata'	S,C,NP
101	Deutzia	S

102	Erica carnea 'Aurea', 'Foxhollow', 'King George', 'Myretoun Ruby', 'Springwood Pink', 'Springwood White', 'Vivelli'	Li
103	Erica darieyensis 'Arthur Johnson'	
104	Erica tetralix 'Alba Mollis'	
105	Erica vagans 'Mrs. D. F. Maxwell'	
106	Erica watsonii 'Dawn'	
107	Eriobotrya deflexa	L
108	Eriobotrya japonica	Li
109	Escallonia exoniensis 'Fradesii'	MG
110	Eucalyptus polyanthemos	Li
111	Euryops pectinatus	MG,S
112	Feijoa sellowiana	L
113	Fig 'Brown Turkey', 'Genoa', 'Kadota', 'Osborne Prolific'	L
114	Forsythia intermedia	MG
115	Fothergilla	
116	Fothergilla monticola	Li
117	Fraxinus oxycarpa 'Raywood'	NP
118	Fremontodendron	MG
119	Gelsemium sempervirens	
120	Genista lydia	S
121	Ginko biloba 'Autumn Gold'	VT
122	Hebe 'Veronica Lake'	MG,VG
123	Hedera helix 'Needlepoint'	R
124	Heteromeles arbutifolia	S

125	Hosta	R
126	Houttuynia cordata	PR
127	Hydrangea quercifolia	R
128	Hypericum 'Hidcote'	PR
129	Ilex crenata 'Dwarf Pagoda', 'Green Dragon'	R
130	Juglans nigra	L
131	Juniperus chinensis 'Old Gold', Pfitzeriana Aurea', 'Sea Green', 'Spearmint', Tolulosa'	R,Ci,S
132	Juniperus sabina 'Arcadia', 'Buffalo', 'Tamariscifolia New Blue'	S
133	Kerria japonica	NP
134	Kiwi	NP
135	Koelreuteria paniculata	VT
136	Larix kaempferi	C
137	Lavendula angustifolia 'Hidcote'	NP
138	Lavendula stoechas	NP
139	Leucothoe Fontanesiana 'Rainbow'	MG
140	Ligustrum japanicum 'Texanum'	PR
141	Liquidambar styraciflua 'Burgundy', 'Festival', seedling 'Palo Alto'	PR,L,NP
142	Lirodendron tulipfera	NP
143	Lithocarpus densiflorus	L
144	Loropetalum chinense	S

145	Magnolia 'Caerhays Belle'	NP,Li,C
146	Magnolia 'Columbus'	NP
147	Magnolia cylindrica	R
148	Magnolia denudata	S
149	Magnolia 'Galaxy'	MG,Li
150	Magnolia grandiflora 'Sammuel Somer'	Li
151	Magnolia 'Iolanthe'	C
152	Magnolia Kosar and De Vos hybrids 'Ann', 'Betty', 'Susan'	NP,MG
153	Magnolia liliflora	MG,R
154	Magnolia loebneri 'Ballerina', 'Leonard Messel'	PR
155	Magnolia 'Picture'	C
156	Magnolia salicifolia 'Miss Jack'	VG
157	Magnolia 'Serenity'	C
158	Magnolia soulangiana seedlings	C
159	Magnolia 'Spectrum'	MG
160	Magnolia springeri 'Diva'	R
161	Magnolia 'Star Wars'	VT
162	Magnolia stellata 'Centennial', 'Royal Star', 'Waterlily'	MG,R
163	Magnolia 'Wada's Memory'	C
164	Magnolia wilsoni 'Bovee'	C
165	Malus 'Dolgo' floribunda, 'Hopa', ioensis 'Plena' (Bechtel), 'Oekomomierat Echtermeyer', 'Pink Spires', 'Radiant', 'Red Silver', 'Royalty', 'Silver Chalice', zumi calocarpa, alba, nigra	MG,VG,VT
166	Maytenus boaria	L
167	Miscanthus	
168	Myrica californica	MG

169	Myosotis (Forget-me not)	MG
170	Nandina domestica seedlings, cultivars	R
171	Nelumbo Mucifera	R
172	Nymphaea	C
173	Nyssa sylvatica	VT,R
174	Olea europea 'Manzanillo'	Li
175	Paeonia suffricosa cultivars	PR,R,S,C
176	Parrotia persica	R
177	Peach cultivars	L
178	Pear 'Bartlett', 'California', 'Comice', 'Max Red Bartlett'	NP,L
179	Pear (Asian cultivars) 'Chojuro', 'Hosui', 'Kikusui', 'Nijiseiki', 'Shinko', 'Shinseiki'	NP,L
180	Persimmon 'Chocolate', 'Fuyu', 'Giant Fuyu', 'Hachiya'	Li,L
181	Philadelphus virginalis	S,MG
182	Photinia frasert	VT,S,CT
183	Phyllostachys aurea, Golden Bamboo	L,C,MG
184	Picea abies 'Nidiformis'	R
185	Picea glauca 'conica' (dwarf Alberta)	PR,S,R,C,Li
186	Picea omorica	R
187	Picea pungens 'Hoopsi', 'Montgomery'	MG
188	Pieris forestii 'Bright Red'	MG
189	Pieris japonica 'Variegata'	MG,C
190	Pinus aristata	S
191	Pinus attenuata	S,L

192	Pinus coulteri	S
193	Pinus densiflora 'Umbraculifera'	R,VT
194	Pinus eldarica	L
195	Pinus halapensis, 'Brutia'	L
196	Pinus jeffreyi	L
197	Pinus lambertiana	L
198	Pinus mugo	S
199	Pinus muricata	L
200	Pinus ponderosa	L
201	Pinus ponderosa x jeffreyi	L
202	Pinus radiata	L
203	Pinus thunbergiana	L
204	Pinus torreyana	L
205	Pinus wallichiana	L
206	Pistacia chinensis	VG
207	Pittosporum eugenioides	Li
208	Platanus acerifolia 'Bloodgood'	R
209	Plum 'Elephant Heart', 'Green Gage', 'Late Santa Rosa', 'Santa Rosa'	L
210	Polygala	
211	Polystichum	NP
212	Pomegranite	C
213	Populus nigra 'Italica'	R
214	Potentilla fruiticosa 'Abbottswood', 'Hollandia Gold', 'Primrose Beauty'	NP,S
215	Prune "Early French', 'Italian', 'Sugar'	L
216	Prunus serrulata (flowering cherry)	NP

217	Prunus serrulata (flowering cherry) 'Bene Hoshio,' 'Kwanzan', 'Shirofugen'	C,L
218	Prunus serrulata (flowering cherry) 'Royal Burgundy', 'Shogetsu', 'Taiwan', 'Okame'	R
219	Prunus subhirtella (flowering cherry), double pink	NP
220	Prunus subhirtella (flowering cherry), single pink, white	
221	Prunus cerasifera (flowering plum) 'Krauter Vesuvius'	R
222	Pseuotsuga menziesii	L
223	Pterocarya fraxinifolia	Li
224	Punica granatum 'Wonderful'	C
225	Pyracantha 'Mohave'	S
226	Pyrus calleryana 'Bradford', 'Capital', 'Redspire'	VG
227	Pyrus salicifolia 'Pendula'	L,R
228	Quercus kelloggii	L
229	Quercus coccinea	NP
230	Quercus rubra	R
231	Quercus wislizenii	NP
232	Rhamnus alaternus	VT
233	Rhododendron	

Note: Since identification tags on the rhododendrons have deteriorated, precise identification has become difficult.

*Rhododendron hybrid 'Alice Bedford', 'America', 'Anah Krushke', 'Anna', 'Anna Rose Whitney', 'Antoon van Welie', 'Autumn Gold', 'Belle Heller', 'Bill Massey', 'Black Prince', 'Blue Diamond', 'Blue Jay', 'Blue Peter', 'Blue Rhapsody', 'Bow Bells',

'Bread and Butter', 'California Blue', 'Chinoides', 'Christmas Cheer', 'Confection', 'County of York', 'Crest', 'Cynthia', 'Dame Nellie Melba', 'Dancing', 'Lady', 'Daphnoides', 'Dora Amateis', 'Dr. Anrold W. Endtz', 'Dr. Bloch',
'El Camino', 'Elizabeth Red Foliage', 'Roseum', Eureka Maid', 'Everstianum', 'Fatuosum Flore Pleno', 'Fort Bragg Glow', 'Full Moon', 'Furnivall's Daughter', 'Gartendirektor Glocker', 'Goldsworth Crimson', 'Gomer Waterer', 'Graf Zepplin', 'Halfdan Lem', 'Hardijzer's Beauty', 'Ice Cube', 'Inheritance', 'Jean Marie de Montague', 'Jim Drewery', 'John Coutts', 'Johnny Bender', 'Kluis Sensation', 'Lady Clemintine Mitford', 'Lady de Rothschild', 'Lee's Dark Purple', 'Lem's 45', 'Loder's White', 'Loderi Game Chick', 'Lord Roberts', 'Marchoness of Lansdowne', 'Margaret Mack', 'Markeeta's Flame', 'Markeeta's Prize', 'Mary
Fleming', 'Molly Ann', 'Mother of Pearl', 'Mrs. Betty Robertson', 'Mrs. Charles E. Pearson', 'Mrs. G. W. Leak', 'Mrs. J. G. Millais', 'Mrs. T. H. Lowinsky', 'Noyo Brave', 'Noyo Chief', 'Ooh Gina', 'Paprika Spiced', 'Petterpot', 'Phyllis Korn', 'Pink Delight', 'Pink Pearl', 'Pink Walloper', 'P. J. M.', 'Point Defiance','Praecox',
'Prairie Fire', 'President Roosevelt', 'Puget Sound', 'Purple Splendor', 'Radium', 'Red Eye', 'Red Olympia', 'Rocket', 'Roseum Elegans', 'Rosy Dream', 'Royal Purple', 'Rubicon', 'Ruby Bowman',
'Sabrina Alder', 'Sappho', 'Scarlet Wonder', 'Scintillation', 'September Song', 'Seta', 'Snow Lady', 'Spitfire', 'Taurus', 'Travis L.', 'Trilby', 'Trude Webster', 'Umpqua Chief', 'Unique', 'Virgo', 'Vulcan', 'Vulcan's Flame', 'Walloper "D"',
'White Swan', 'Yellow Hammer' NP,MG,C,Li,S

234   Rhododendron kaempferi hybrids
235   Rhododendron maddenii hybrids 'Actress', 'Alice Eastwood', 'Bill Massey', 'Butterhorn', 'California Gold', 'Conchita', 'Countess of Haddington', 'Eldorado', 'Else Frye', 'Fostertanum',

'Heaven Scent', 'Lake Lorraine', 'Lemon Mist', 'Meadowgold', 'Mi Amor', 'My Lady', 'Muriel Glaique', 'Mysterious Maddenii', 'Rose Scott', 'Sabrina Alder', 'Saffron Prince', 'Scott Maddenii', 'Scott's Valentine' NP,MG,S

236 Rhododendron Mollis hybrids

237 Rhododendron augustinii, Barto Blue form MG

238 Rhododendron catawbiense 'Album' MG

239 Rhododendron 'Boursault' MG

240 Rhododendron cubitti MG

241 Rhododendron formosum

242 Rhododendron klusianum

243 Rhododendron maddenii g. Langois

244 Rhododendron odoriferum

245 Rhododendron oreotrephies

246 Rhododendron ponticum dark form, light form MG

247 Rhododendron taronense

248 Rhododendron vietchianum

249 Rhododendron yakushimanum
'Ken Janeck', 'Phetteplace (tall form)', 'Yaku Angel'

250 Rhododendron (evergreen Azaleas) S,MG
'Alaska', 'Ama Gasa', 'Beni Kirishima', 'Blue Danube', 'Brilliant', 'Buccaneer', 'Caroline Gable', 'Casablanca', 'Dorothy Gish', 'Double Beauty', 'Duc de Rohan', 'Eikan', 'Everest', 'Fielder's White', 'Flame Creeper', 'Formosa' (Phoenicia), 'Geisha Girl', 'George Lindley Taber', 'Glacier', 'Glamour', 'Glory of Sunninghill', 'Gumpo Pink', 'Gumpo White', 'Hahn's Red', 'Helen Close', 'Hexe', 'Higasa', 'Hino-crimson', 'Hinodegiri', 'Kaempo', 'Louise Gable', 'Macrantha', 'Martha Hitchcock', 'Mother's Day', 'Mucronatum', 'Murasaki Shikibu',

'Osakazuki', 'Polypetalum', 'Pride of Dorking', 'Purple Splendor', 'Redwing', 'Rosaflora', 'Rosebud', 'Rukizon', 'Sakuragata', 'Sherwood Red', 'Sherwood Orchid', 'Shinnyo no Tsuki', 'Snow Mound', 'Southern Charm', 'Stewartsonian', 'Vuyk's Rosy Red', 'Vuyk's Scarlet', 'Ward's Ruby'

251	Rhododendron (deciduous Azaleas)	C,MG,Li
252	Rhus typhina	
253	Ribes sanguineum 'King Edward VII'	NP
254	Ribes speciosum	NP
255	Robinia pseudoaccacia 'Frisia'	MG,L
256	Rosa hybrid 'About Face, 'Angel Face', 'Blue Girl', 'Brandy', 'Burgundy Iceberg', 'China Doll', 'Chinois', 'Chrysler Imperial', 'Clutterbye', Chris Evert,' 'Double Delight', 'Easy Going', 'Europeana', 'Fragrant Cloud', 'Gold Medal', 'Graceland', 'Helmut Schmidt', 'Iceberg', 'In the Mood', 'Julia Child', 'Livin' Easy', 'Moonstone', 'Lavaglut', 'Mr. Lincoln', 'Ole', 'Olympiad', 'Oregold', 'Robin Hood', 'Sarabande', 'Strike It Rich', 'Sun Flare', 'Sunsprite', 'The Fairy', 'Trumpeter', 'Wild Blue Yonder'	
257	Rosa arkansa	L
258	Rosa chinensis 'Manetti'	L
259	Rosa davidii	L
260	Rosa eglanteria	VP
261	Rosa rugosa 'Rubra'	L
262	Rosmarinue officinalis	NP,S
263	Rubus deliciosus	MG
264	Salix babylonica	S
265	Salix matsudana 'Tortuosa'	PR
266	Sambucus caerulea	
267	Saptum sebiferum	NP

268	Sarcocca ruscifolia	R
269	Sequoia sempervirens 'Albo-Spica', 'Aptos Blue', 'Santa Cruz', 'Soquel', seedlings	L
270	Sequoiadendron giganteum	L
271	Skimmia japonica	MG
272	Sophora japonica	VT
273	Spiraea vanhouttei	S
274	Stewartia koreana	MG
275	Stewartia pseudocamellia	MG
276	Styrax japonicus	MG,VG
277	Syringa reticulata	MG,C
278	Syringa vulgaris 'Charles Joly'	MG
279	Taxodium distichum	S
280	Taxus baccata 'Fastigata'	L
281	Tasus media 'Kelseyi'	VG
282	Thuja occidentalis 'Emerald', 'Rhinegold', 'Sherwood Moss', 'Stoneham Gold'	R
283	Tibouchina urvilleana	C
284	Tilia cordata	
285	Torreya californica	R
286	Trachelospermium jasmoides	MG,R
287	Umbellularia californica	L
288	Vaccinium ovatum	L
289	Vibrunum davidii	C

290	Vibrunum plicatum tomentosum 'Shasta', 'Pink Beauty'	R
291	Vibrunum tinus 'Spring Bouquet'	R
292	Vinca major	C
293	Vinca minor	NP
294	Walnut (Juglans regia) 'Amigo', 'Carmello', 'Franquette', 'Hartley'	L
295	Weigelia florida 'Variegata'	R

Location Key

C	=Chapel	CT	=Cintamani environs
Li	=Anandabhadra Library	VT	=Vajra Temple environs
MG	=Mandala Garden	PR	=Pilgrimage Road
R	=Rim	L	=Out on the land
S	=Stupa	VG	=Vairocana Garden
NP	=North Park		

Wisteria floribunda japonica,
'Longissima Alba', purple, pink, blue   C,R

Wisteria sinensis 'Caroline' blue, pink, 'Cook's Double Purple', white   R

Odiyan Gardens (Summary)

Inside the perimeter fence	144 acres
Vegetable garden	1.5 acres
Orchards	14 acres
Tibet Hill Garden	3 acres
Yeshe Tsogyal Lake Garden	1 acre
Rhododendron Forest	2 acres
Cherry Mall	14 acres
Mandala Garden	4.5 acres
Arbor Garden	1 acre
North Park Garden	2.5 acres
Stupa and Peace Gardens	4.5 acres
Vajra Bell (Vairocana) Garden	2 acres
Stupa Road plantings	1.5 acres
Vajra Temple Garden	2 acres
Vajra Temple environs	8 acres
Rim Gardens	4 acres

Chapel Garden	1 acre
Head Lama's Garden	1 acre
Redwood Meadow	1 acre
Azalea Forest	2 acres

A Life Devoted to Dharma Activity

Tarthang Tulku, also known as
Kunga Gellek Yeshe Dorje,
was born in Golok, Eastern Tibet, in 1935.

Thoroughly trained by traditional masters, he went into exile in 1958. After a short stay at the Young Lamas Home School in Dalhousie, he was asked by H.H. Dudjom Rinpoche to represent the Nyingma School at Sanskrit University in Varanasi. There he established Dharma Mudranalaya to print Tibetan Buddhist texts. In 1968 he left India for the United States, becoming the first Nyingma lama in America.

In 1969, Rinpoche founded the Tibetan Nyingma Meditation Center (TNMC), a California corporation sole, as the nucleus of his activities.

He established Padma Ling as a residential center, and in 1972–73 founded the Nyingma Institute, where he taught publicly until 1978. During these years he published the first of his 34 books in English to aid students in their study. He also founded the Tibetan Aid Project to support Tibetans in exile; Dharma Press and Dharma Publishing, which have now printed and produced hundreds of art reproductions and more than 130 books in Western languages; Nyingma Centers, to guide the growth of four international centers; and Odiyan Country Center, a mandala of temples, stupas, and libraries, including Vajra Temple, Cintamani Temple, the Enlightenment Stupa, and Vairocana Garden; Ratna Ling Retreat Center, established in 2004 as an adjunct to Odiyan, offers retreats to the general public.

In 1981, Rinpoche published the *Nyingma Edition of the Tibetan Buddhist Canon* in 120 atlas-sized volumes, followed by an eight-volume Catalogue and Bibliography. The Yeshe De Text Project, founded in 1983, produced *Great Treasures of Ancient Teachings* in 641 volumes, and has printed and distributed to the Tibetan community over five million books, including five versions of the Kanjur and three versions of the Tanjur. In its latest edition, the Yeshe De Kanjur is the most comprehensive collection ever assembled, and includes 12 historically significant karchags, or catalogues. Yeshe De is currently producing the most rare and comprehensive collection of Nyingma Tantras ever compiled, in 150 volumes.

In 1989 Rinpoche founded the Nyingma Monlam Chenmo (World Peace Ceremony) in Bodh Gaya, where 8–10,000 lamas, monks, and nuns gather annually. He also provided seed money to initiate the Kagyu, Sakya and Gelug Monlams. Since 1989, 5 million sacred books, 3.25 million sacred art images, and 176,250 prayer wheels have been distributed to more than 3,300 Dharma centers in India, Nepal, Bhutan and Tibet. A total of 66,285 copies of the precious 8,000-line Prajnaparamita including this year's offering to the 2017 Monlam of 414 engraved granite plaques in Sanskrit, Tibetan and English, 100 decorative victory banners and six important editions in large poti format have been offered to the Sangha. Other offerings for Bodh Gaya include six butter lamp houses, 152 prayer wheels, 158 golden lhantsa and Tibetan Prajnaparamita plaques, support towards the restoration the Mahabodhi Temple spire, site beautification, and year-round offerings of butterlamps.

In 2002 he founded the Light of Buddhadharma Foundation to support annual Tipitaka Chanting Ceremonies by the Theravadin Sangha, both in Bodh Gaya and around the world; representatives from 12 countries now participate.

Rinpoche's centers have installed sixteen 2½ ton World Peace Bells at holy places, and have supported renovation projects at sacred sites, including the historic renovation of the Swayambhu Stupa in Nepal.

In 2005 Mangalam Light Foundation was established; operating through Ananda, Prajna, and Vajra Light Foundations, its mission is to revive, preserve, and support the heritage of the Buddha Dharma in Tibet. The Light Foundations have given substantial support to Tarthang Monastery, Larun Gar, Chokyab Gar, and Adzom Gar among other centers and over 1,000 sets of the Kanjur and 10,000 sets of the collected works of Kun khyen Longchenpa are being distributed to monasteries throughout Tibet.

In 2009, Rinpoche founded the Mangalam Research Center for Buddhist Languages in downtown Berkeley, followed by Dharma College and the Guna Foundation, a documentary film-making unit.

In 2013, he inaugurated Sarnath International Nyingma Institute to bridge the gap between East and West, support the study of the Khen Lob Cho Sum, and host the annual Tibet Peace Ceremony. The Nyingma Association of Mandala Organizations (NAMO) incorporated in 2012, helps guide and protect the work of its 17 member organizations.

Rinpoche has dedicated his life to preserve, protect, and distribute the Tibetan Buddhist heritage and manifest the sacred forms of kaya, vaca, citta, guna, and karma for the sake of the entire world. We cannot express all of his efforts here, but more information on the mandala's activities is recorded in the 45 volumes of the TNMC Annals.

Sarvam Mangalam
October 1, 2016